Love Lessons

Love Lessons

22 Keys to a Life of Legendary Love

Terry McDonald

Bliss 42 Media

Fairhope, Alabama

Terry McDonald

Fairhope, Alabama

www.Bliss42Media.com

Terry@bliss42media.com

Love Lessons/Terry McDonald – First Edition
ISBN: 0988608820
ISBN-13:978-0988608825

CONTENTS

"Three things will last forever—faith, hope, and love— and the greatest of these is love."

—1 Corinthians 13:13

Preface

The quality of the love relationships in your life is the single most important predictor of your overall satisfaction in life.

"My research showed that love is by far the most important resource in people's lives. It relates most to happiness."

—Dr. Robert M. Gordon

The significance of this is hard to overstate. You can be well educated, wealthy, and praised by millions and still be unhappy and unfulfilled because you have not addressed your genuine love needs. How many Hollywood stars with millions of fans who are rich, beautiful, and in rehab does it take to underscore this point?

On the other hand, you can have a limited but adequate education, modest income, a limited lifestyle, the respect and admiration of the few people you really care about, and a fulfilling love relationship and feel happy and complete.

Think about how much time, energy, and money people invest to acquire the education, wealth, and acclaim they want, and then consider how much care, attention, time, and effort is put into becoming a world-class lover.

The results in the general population are obvious when you consider the statistics of love.

A typical rating scale:

The left side of this scale represents someone very dissatisfied with his or her love relationship. The center is neither satisfied nor dissatisfied, and the extreme right is very satisfied.

A depressingly high number of people have love relationships that are to the left of center. The divorce rate tells us that half of all people who marry are the frowny- faced guy on the extreme left. How many more married and unmarried people are also in this category? How many more are not very dissatisfied but are still dissatisfied, which is represented by the second face from the left? How many more have arrived at a truce or accommodation and might be friends and are neither satisfied nor dissatisfied as represented by the emoticon in the middle? How many would like to divorce but do not for religious, financial, social, or other reasons? When you do all of the math, the category on the extreme right by one calculation may include as few as 16 percent of all couples.

If you agree that the quality of your love relationship and the quality of your life as a whole are highly connected, then making it into the 16 percent group is the only way to go. The good news is that membership in this group is not limited. There is room enough for everyone. I do realize that as more and more people attain and maintain this "happy in love" state, the 16 percent label will no longer apply. I am labeling the 16 percent group today as the "Legendary Lovers" in anticipation of and hope for the day when that percentage will be much higher.

This book is all about getting into and remaining in the Legendary Lovers group. As a matter of fact, it is about getting into the upper end of that group and pushing the envelope from there.

Four different kinds of readers are likely to benefit from this book in different ways.

The first is someone who has never had a long-term relationship and wants to get it right from the start. If you are part of this group, every part of this book will apply to you, but my concern is that you might not have experienced enough pain and suffering to take everything in this book seriously.

The second group consists of veterans who are currently single, with the purple hearts to prove it. You are much more likely to take the book seriously and to do the things that require years of effort to get right.

The third group consists of people in troubled relationships right now. Pain is a great motivator, and you may find something in this book that will help to heal and grow your relationship.

The fourth group consists of people who are in a positive, loving relationship now and who want to nurture and develop that relationship and take it to even greater heights. This group will be able to validate a lot of conclusions in the book, and they will gain confidence that they are on the right track. They also might pick up a few tips that will help them in their journey.

This book was written in the hope that many more people will experience a legendary love relationship and the bliss that comes from it. I hope that you, dear reader, either are or soon will be one of   them.

PART ONE

From Love-Worthy to Love-Ready

Everyone is "Love-Worthy" (OK, maybe we can all think of a few exceptions), but many are not "Love-Ready."

There is a saying that luck happens when preparation meets opportunity. A deeply loving relationship starts when two well-matched, Love-Ready people meet and recognize each other.

In part one, you will learn about how this book came to be, why being Love-Ready is so important, and the work needed to get Love-Ready.

How and Why This Book Was Written

My wife said to me, "Write a book about how to love a woman. It is what you know best. It is what you do best." She was drawing on over three decades of intimate knowledge, so I thought she ought to know what she was talking about. As always, I took her advice seriously, and so this book was born.

The two of us make time for conversation daily. This has been a source of strength in our relationship from the beginning. We constantly renew our relationship and chart our future together during these conversations. These conversations have led us to radically change our lifestyle and business several times. Together we have bet the ranch on new ways to live and work, and together we have created a life that gives us both joy and deep satisfaction.

We share everything from the mundane details of our day to profound thoughts about life and love. Any decision that will impact our life together is always talked through.

The conversation that led to this book began with my confession that I was frustrated. Despite a long, wonderful, and varied career, I felt as if I had not done my most important work yet. I felt as though I had been preparing all my life for something and was now ready for it, but I did not know what that something was.

When she said to me, "Write a book about how to love a woman. It is what you know best. It is what you do best," three things struck me immediately. The first was a feeling of elation. Loving my wife has been a priority for me from the beginning. Her affirmation that I was doing it well made me feel like a total success. The second thought was stark terror. I'm not Oprah or Dr. Phil, so why would anyone want to read what I have to say about love? It also occurred to me that to write the book well, I would have to open my life to the world in ways that might be very uncomfortable. The third thought was that there are surely men out there who do a much better job of loving their wives than me. The I thought but who among them would be crazy enough to write about it?

What got me to go forward was the thought that perhaps one or more people might find something in this book that would bring some love and joy into their lives and into their partners' lives. The more I thought about that possibility, the more I started to believe that perhaps this is what I had been preparing for and working toward my whole life.

For ten years I tried to make an unsuccessful marriage work, and for over thirty years I have been continuously striving to better love the woman of my dreams in a blissfully happy marriage. Both experiences have taught me lessons, and these are the "Love Lessons."

I learned these lessons through trial and error. The errors vastly outnumbered the successes. The learning process was messy and chaotic and not neatly organized into twenty-two lessons. I got up each day and tried to love the best I could that day. There were no blinding flashes of insight. There were only small, incremental gains on most days and setbacks on others.

Nietzsche said, among a lot of other things, that "life can only be understood backward, but unfortunately it can only be lived forward."

The process of writing this book forced me to look backward. By looking backward, I could see clearly the things that had been very unclear as I lived them forward. Looking backward, the twenty-two lessons in this book came into sharp focus.

You might be tempted to see the twenty-two lessons as a prescription. They are not. The essence of a lesson can be applied very differently by different people to match the unique personality and needs they and their partner have. Some of the lessons will fit with your life today and perhaps some tomorrow. It is conceivable that some will never be a fit.

This is a book for people who want to establish and continually grow a deeply loving and satisfying relationship. While I wrote it from my perspective—a man's—my female reviewers report that they can read it from a woman's perspective just as easily. My hope is that all sorts of lovers read it for themselves and take from it something good for them.

As you read this book, the important thoughts are not the ones I wrote but the ones you have while reading. Keep a notebook handy and capture your own thoughts. Toward the end of the book, I will have some suggestions on how to turn your notes into an improved life for you and your current or future partner.

"In school, you're taught a lesson and then given a test.

In life, you're given a test that teaches you a lesson."

—Tom Bodett

Love Lesson One

Mistakes Hurt Others Too

Marital bliss was not always my lot in life. I got married the first time when I was too young and too inexperienced to know what I wanted and truly needed. I also had not yet dealt with my own neuroses, and therefore I had no business getting married.

One of the biggest problems with being young and foolish is that your youth and foolishness prevent you from knowing just how young and foolish you are. Older and wiser people tried desperately to talk me out of marrying so young. One of my brothers even threatened to stand on the steps of the church and wrestle me to the ground if that was what was necessary. I knew better than all of them, and so the wedding went forward.

The problem with my mistake is that many people besides me suffered as a result. My daughter has told me that the breakup and all that it entailed put her through an extremely rough time. My ex, our parents, and relatives and friends were also put through things they did not deserve. I did not fully appreciate the potential for all of this "collateral damage" before I got married despite watching some pretty spectacular and nasty divorces. With the benefit of 20/20 hindsight, I can clearly see now that the choice to marry someone is the most important decision a person can make, and therefore it merits very careful consideration. I deeply regret my mistake, and I apologize for the pain I caused to many people who deserved better.

Three good things did come from my first marriage. First is the daughter whom I love, respect, admire, and cannot imagine not having in my life. Second is a set of lessons learned that serve me very well in my current marriage. Much of what I will share in this book, I learned in those ten years as I struggled to make a fundamentally flawed marriage work. Finally, all of the events in my life ultimately led me to the lady of my dreams and the marriage I have today.

Pain is a great motivator. During those ten years, I underwent therapy and became a psychotherapist, and for a short time I did marriage counseling, but quickly thought better of it and referred marital cases to others. I taught parenting and interpersonal skills, took a great deal of training, and participated in ongoing group therapy. I read the literature on relationships voraciously, and I wrote articles on conflict management and taught hundreds of conflict management seminars.

I took my knowledge on the road and became a highly successful speaker on the national circuit. This led to consulting work with companies where I helped teams and individuals to improve relationships and, consequently, performance. Everything I learned and taught I also applied in my personal life to try to salvage my marriage, but without success. I now know that all of these skills work well when the match between two people is good, but nothing in my experience fixes a fundamentally bad match.

I am not a quitter. As a matter of fact, I am known to be the human equivalent of a pit bull with a rawhide chew. I attempted to apply everything I was learning to create the kind of marriage I craved and believed possible. Nothing worked. My physical and emotional health began to suffer. It was clear that continuing down the same path would result in me being crazy, a drunk, or dead. I finally surrendered and admitted to myself that my marriage would never work.

One thing I was very sure of after that decade was that I never wanted to be in that kind of a relationship again. I had a vision of the kind of relationship I wanted, and I was bound and determined to make that relationship a reality. I found the love of my life, and she wanted the same thing. We agreed that we would create and maintain a relationship very different from the ones we had in the past.

Wanting something and agreeing to it is much easier than actually doing it. Decade after decade we have done it. We have faced numerous challenges along the way, and together we have overcome them. The circumstances of our lives changed as our kids grew up and went through their own rough patches. We had lean years when credit card advances were needed to pay our tax bill, but we also enjoyed prosperous years. Through the years we have always kept the romance going, and we have always been partners, friends, playmates, companions, and lovers.

We have observed many other relationships in our three-plus decades together. We have noticed that some men and women work very hard at being attractive to each other until they marry. After the wedding, they let their bodies go, they let their grooming go, and they cease to do the things that got them together in the first place. After a few years they break up, immediately join a gym, get a makeover, and start the process again. To us this makes no sense at all. If you have found the love of your life, why not romance this person forever? Why stop striving to look good and smell good for him or her? Why stop bringing home flowers or other surprises, taking him or her on dates, and planning a romantic evening together? Why not keep the magic alive instead of allowing it to fade away?

Preserving the wild passion of newlyweds and establishing the relaxed comfort of long-term marriage while raising children and working as business partners required us to learn and grow continuously. We consider ourselves and our relationship to be a never-ending work in progress.

The lessons we have learned and applied in the real world work for us. They are being shared with you in the hope that some of the ideas will help you and someone you love to have a happier, more fulfilling relationship.

The scientist in me wants to issue a word of caution. When an experiment is conducted, the number of subjects in the experiment is expressed as N. The larger the N, the greater the confidence that the results of the experiment may be applicable to the general population. When $N=1$, great care must be taken with generalization. Strictly speaking, my wife and I are a case study from which you may be able to take a few things of use for yourself. Evaluate carefully what you take and what you leave behind.

That said, the lessons learned that I will share with you are based not only on my own experience but on a lifetime of studying. Love has been written about in religion, philosophy, poetry, music, and science since the time of the ancients. I have devoured vast quantities of this literature. Where appropriate I will point you to sources I have drawn upon so you can go deeper in your own studies if you wish.

I also do not expect everyone to agree with my conclusions. Your life and your desires may be very different from mine. Take from this book the things that are good for you and leave the rest behind. If you believe I am absolutely wrong about something, go to the website www.Bliss42Media.com and leave a comment. You can also post questions and comments at the "Love Lessons" page on Facebook. I welcome disagreement, and I find opposing points of view help me a lot. Questions can also be posted there, and we will do our best to answer them.

*"Just about any **what** is easy if you have a good enough **why**."*

Unknown

Love Lesson Two

You Need a "Why"

What gets you out of bed in the morning? What do you truly care about? What is the meaning and purpose of your life? These are hard questions. You might even shy away from them because they are too hard. The good news is that once you have even tentative answers to these questions, everything else is easier.

Where do you go to find a "why"? Start by asking yourself what you really do care about. If religion is important to you, consider what your religion has to say on the subject of love. Great teachers from Aristotle to Zoroaster (did you get the A–Z thing in there?) have taught about the importance of love. Every world religion holds that love is foundational even if that is not obvious from the behavior of many of its members.

I believe that love is the key to the "good life." I also believe that love can be expressed in lots of ways in lots of different kinds of relationships and that it is all good.

After my father died, my mother poured her love into her children, grandchildren, and great-grandchildren. She made no distinction between blood relatives and step children. She simply loved any member of the family willing to receive her love. My mom's constant companion was her dog, Danny. Clearly she loved him, and he loved her, and that was good too. What kind of love do you want in your life? What fits you best given where you are in your life right now?

For me, my love relationship with my wife is the single most important source of meaning in my life. No matter what else is going on, I wake up each day with something important to do: to love her the best way I know how and to learn something that day that will allow me to love her better tomorrow.

So what do you want from life? Do you want a strong, deep, and blissful relationship? I believe that everyone has the potential to attain this kind of relationship, but it does not come easily or quickly. I do not think such a relationship is possible without a determined and consistent effort over years.

Do you have a good enough "why" to do the work and suffer whatever is necessary to attain love in your life? Do you have a good enough "why" to take action daily and consistently to nurture and grow a love relationship?

Do you have a strong enough "why" to engage in the kind of self-improvement that will make you the man of her dreams when you meet the woman of your dreams? Or the kind of self-improvement that will make you the woman of his dreams when you meet the man of your dreams?

From the above it would be easy to conclude that the process of bringing love into your life is nothing but an ordeal. It is not. It is a journey. Like any journey, there can be both pleasant and unpleasant surprises and moments. Like any journey, it involves putting one foot in front of the other and moving forward whenever possible. The key is to embrace and enjoy the journey. The ideal of a perfect relationship is useful for navigating the journey. It is like the North Star; it keeps you pointed in the right direction. The journey never ends, and the destination is never achieved, so it is important to take joy from each step along the way, to learn from the times you get lost or stumble. Do not allow yourself to get caught up in the trap of believing that you will be happy when you arrive at the destination, because this belief means that you will not be happy along the way.

Dealing with the doubts and concerns that might inhibit you is also important. Some of you may have a problem with the idea of putting your spouse in the number one position. What about god or the kids? you might say. For me the answer is easy. Placing my wife first allows me to create a well of love that I can draw upon and she can draw upon. The love I give her multiplies and creates a surplus that flows over into all aspects of our lives.

When you read the suggestions in this book, you might think that you have to be some kind of selfless masochist who always puts the other person first at your expense. The paradox is that the more you give to the other person, the more you have and the more you get.

Sometimes you get quid pro quo, as in the case of bringing her coffee in bed one day and her bringing you coffee in bed the next. While this is nice when it happens, it is not the point. There is great joy in simply giving love. The reward is immediate and requires nothing from the other person. When you fill the other person with love, he or she naturally wants to return the favor, so in addition to the bliss of giving love, there is an abundant second reward of your loved one doing the same for you. Giving love, therefore, is not an act of self-sacrifice. It is actually a very selfish thing to do.

Filling the other person with love to the point of overflowing brings other benefits as well. Your loved one will have ample love to give to you and plenty more to give to your children, parents, and others in need of love. This in turn makes your home and your circle of family and friends more enjoyable and may also result in giving to charitable causes that help to solve problems and improve the lives of strangers.

We have seen the opposite of this phenomenon in dysfunctional couples. In these relationships, both parties spend a lot of time tallying how much they have given and how much they have gotten in return. This attitude creates scarcity and a kind of self-centeredness that is lonely and toxic.

Giving love, therefore, is at once the most generous and the most selfish act you can perform. It creates an atmosphere of abundance. It gives life meaning and makes any "what" bearable.

I wish I believed that this would work with any two random people, but life experience has taught me otherwise. There are people in the world who are pure takers and who will suck the soul out of a giver. If you are a giver, you will encounter these people from time to time. Feel sorry for these people, but safeguard yourself from them to avoid being dragged down by them.

Another aspect of this paradox is that you cannot give something you do not have. Self-love and self-respect are preconditions for giving love and respect to others. Some of the worst things people do can be traced to their lack of self-worth, insecurity, and neediness. If someone is behaving badly, a close examination will almost always find deep insecurity and lack of self-worth at the root.

It is also possible to give too much, deplete yourself, and become needy and resentful. I have seen parents do this and then be angry with the ungrateful brats they are raising. I have seen adults who care for their elderly parents become bitter because they fail to meet their own needs in a way that keeps their love batteries charged.

Burnout is a common problem with givers. The sad thing about givers is that burnout makes them useless to themselves and others. The key is to monitor how much you have "in the tank" and to fill up before running empty.

If you have children, or plan to have children, you will be giving them a huge gift by showing them what a loving couple looks like. My wife and I were both extremely fortunate to have parents who were obviously deeply in love. Their excellent example was and is an inspiration to us.

In case you need any more reasons to build love in your life, here are ten that were listed on MedicineNet.com in an article titled "10 Surprising Health Benefits of Love."

1. Fewer Doctor Visits
2. Less Depression
3. Lower Blood Pressure
4. Less Anxiety
5. Natural Pain Control
6. Better Stress Management
7. Fewer Colds

8. Faster Healing
9. Longer Life
10. Happier Life

When you look at this list, it should become clear that we are wired at the most fundamental level in mind, body, and spirit to be lovers. Is there a more powerful "why"?

*"Is there anyone
so wise as to learn
by the experience
of others?"*

—Voltaire

Love Lesson Three

Choose Carefully and Well

It all starts with who you select as the love of your life. This is probably the most important life choice you will make. Every aspect of your life will be impacted by this decision. If you choose badly and end the relationship, there will be fallout and injured parties. There is no escaping the magnitude of this decision.

Most relationships are the result of chance. You meet a tiny percentage of the billions of people on earth, and very few of the people you meet are potential lovers.

You are likely to be interested in potential partners in a certain age range, of a certain gender, who are single, and interested in a relationship. You might have other strong preferences regarding religion, height, weight, education, and other qualities that narrow the list quite a bit.

Most people know very few people. Most of the people they know come from their immediate community, school, work, or other closed environment. What are the odds of finding the ideal love partner in a small circle of people who are mostly too old, young, the wrong gender or sexual orientation, or in some other way unsuitable for a long, deeply loving relationship with you?

Math professor Peter Backus used the Drake equation to determine how many women in the UK were possible matches for him. He determined that there were probably only twenty-six women who would be suitable. On a night out in London, he calculated that he would have a one in 285,000 chance of meeting one of those twenty-six women. Backus published the results of his analysis in a paper titled "Why I don't have a girlfriend" in 2010. Backus met and married the woman of his dreams in 2013.

With odds that bad, it is not unusual for two people who are not ideally suited to each other to start dating, move to dating exclusively, and, after a while, get engaged and then married. Drifting together in this fashion involves a lot of small decisions that end up being a huge decision. The progression of small steps does not seem like much until you wake up married one day. You might be lucky and find the love of your life in the small subset of humanity most of us are exposed to, or you might find a bad match and drift into a bad long-term relationship by default.

This was the way my first marriage occurred. I know there are many millions of people who got married this way and remain happily married today, but given the consequences of getting it wrong, doesn't it make sense to be a little more deliberate about the process?

Begin with self-knowledge

Informed choice requires that you know yourself first. Good self-knowledge is not easy to come by. In most cases this knowledge is acquired in the school of hard knocks. Some people are sufficiently introspective that they will delve into their own psyche to extract self-knowledge, but these are the exceptions. As a minimum, you will need to know what you value. Values are the things we prize and cherish. What do you prize and cherish?

What are the top ten things you value? No matter how cute, smart, charming, or whatever a man or woman is, if he or she is 180 degrees out from you on your core values, trouble will brew.

If, for example, you prize and cherish your extended family, then the man or woman of your dreams would need to be someone with the desire and ability to build bonds with your family and who would enjoy spending time with them. If he or she is not so inclined, you will find yourself perpetually torn between him or her and your desire for your family.

What are your dreams? What kind of life do you want to have one, five, ten, or more years from now? What kind of sacrifices will you and your partner have to make to produce the future you desire? A compatible set of dreams and a joint willingness to do the things necessary to attain them prevents a lot of fighting.

What role will your career play in your life? I have known men who were intent on becoming CEO of a large company and who would do almost anything to attain that goal. Women might like the idea of the prestige and money involved, but many of them become jealous of the company that gets top priority. Other women are strongly supportive and are interested in being teammates in the attainment of the goal. Alternatively she may want to be the CEO, and you will need to be the supporter who helps her to attain that target. Are you ready for that?

My career was a strain on me and my wife. The nature of my work required extensive travel and separation. We survived those years because we were on the same page about what I was doing and why I was doing it. My wife became an integral part of the business, so she saw both sides of the ledger and knew why I had to be away. We talked about the strain and considered other options, but finally we decided that the work I was doing was the best for us.

Because we were in total agreement, we were able to then change the focus to how to make our lifestyle work for us. We were blessed with fabulous parents who helped by staying with our children and thus made it possible for us to travel together occasionally for work and much-needed "just the two of us" vacations.

Do you want children? If so, when? We had our kids when we were young. Friends and family members who chose to have children later in life have had very different life experiences from us. Couples we know who elected to have no children or to adopt also had very different lives from us. It is useful to consider which of these options is right for you. There are pros and cons to each. Problems occur when you fall in love and discover later that the two of you have very different ideas of what the decision regarding children should be.

How important is money to you? Are you the kind of person who can happily get by with a simple, inexpensive lifestyle? Do you want to accumulate significant wealth? Do you want a lot of "stuff"? Money may or may not be the root of all evil, but it definitely is the root of many couple fights and breakups.

One study of 2,800 couples showed a strong positive correlation between the frequency of arguments over money and divorce. The more often these couples disagreed about money, the more likely it was that they would divorce.

Know your weaknesses and neuroses

It also helps to know you weaknesses and fears and the parts of your psyche that are a bit out of whack. People with feelings of inadequacy or poor self-image are easy prey for those who exploit weaknesses. Sadly, many twisted but strong bonds are formed between people with neurotic needs. Psychoanalyst Karen Horney—yes, psych students chuckle when her name is introduced—lists ten neurotic needs that are exaggerations of normal human needs that can serve to create an unhealthy bond between two people.

Here is an abbreviated list of the ten neurotic needs she identified:

1. Low self-worth and an exaggerated need for approval from others.

2. Seeking a partner who will be the solution to all problems.

3. Desperately seeking power and control over others.

4. Obsessive need to win at others' expense.

5. Excessive desire to acquire things to attain social acceptance.

6. Desire to be esteemed by others as an ideal.

7. Achieving in a way that is superior to others.

8. Extreme self-sufficiency.

9. Perfectionism.

10. Restricting life within narrow borders.

Any attempt to reduce a noted psychoanalyst's work to ten lines is inherently flawed, so I encourage you to read her work directly. The point of this list is to help you to see that neurotic needs are very similar to normal needs but are taken to excess. The list can also be used to briefly contemplate how easy it would be for a person with one or more neurotic needs to fall into a relationship that would be fundamentally unhealthy.

If a relationship is formed based on neurotic needs and one party becomes healthier, there is a good chance that the relationship will end. Feeding a neurotic need is like giving drugs to a junkie. Stopping the supply is going to generate a severe withdrawal reaction, which could get ugly. Some neurotics defend and protect their neuroses to the death.

If you are a little neurotic (most of us are), get some counseling and get your head straight first, or you may end up tying yourself into a neurotic knot that even Alexander the Great could not sever. (If the Alexander the Great reference is too obscure, google "Gordian Knot.")

Armed with self-knowledge and a reasonably neurosis-free mind, you are ready to think about the qualities you seek in the love of your life.

How old and experienced do you need to be?

The age at which this stage of life is reached varies greatly. In the United States and other developed parts of the world, it has occurred about a decade later in the last generation and now is about thirty years of age.

This poses an interesting problem. Sexual maturity is being reached earlier and social maturity later. This means that there are somewhere between fifteen and eighteen years during which a person is capable of and motivated to have sex but not mature enough to make many important life decisions. What could possibly go wrong in this scenario?

Many of the dumbest errors in life happen in that fifteen-year period. The obvious solution is to go to a monastery for fifteen years. No? Not an option for you? Then do not make any irreversible decisions during that period. It is a good time to develop your list of musts and wants in a life partner and to test them against the people you date. It is also a good time to clarify your own values, which underlie the "musts" and "wants."

The concept of musts and wants

A must and want list is a tool you can use for getting your head straight about a complex and emotionally charged choice. A well-formed list is a set of smaller decisions that helps you make big decisions when lots of options are possible. Let's pretend you are shopping for a house. What is the most you will consider spending? The answer tells you that all houses you will consider must be priced below that number. What is the minimum square footage that you will consider? Are schools important? If so, which school districts would you consider?

Notice that each decision narrows the field of houses you will even consider. These decisions are made before you look at houses. Setting a ceiling on price prevents you from touring and falling in love with a house you cannot afford, which could prevent foreclosure a few years later. When your list is complete and you look for houses under a certain dollar limit with a certain minimum number of square feet in good school districts, you may discover that there are no houses that meet these criteria on the market.

This is where your time frame comes into play. If you are willing to wait, you may be able to get a house that meets all of your criteria, but if you are rushed, you may have to settle. The must list might also contain must-not's. If, for example, you will not buy a house on a busy street because you do not want the noise or the risk to small children, then "busy street" would go on the must-not list. Must and must-not's are all-or-nothing propositions. If a must is missing or a must-not is present, the deal is dead.

Wants are a different story. You might prefer a French country-style house, but you may not consider it a necessity. In this case, if two houses meet all of the musts and must-not's, and one is a French country, the style that is a "want" would be used to make the final selection between two acceptable options.

Let's apply this concept to prospective life partners. If a person does not have a must, you probably should not date him or her. Likewise with must-not's. If a person does have a must-not, he or she is not date material. Why am I saying that you should not date this person? The reason is simple: you will not marry someone you do not date.

The last sentence sounds a little crazy until you think about it. Let's suppose that you start to date someone because you met her at the beach and she is the type who should wear nothing but bikinis. As a healthy male who appreciates this fine quality, you date her and enjoy her looks and the looks of admiration from your friends. One thing leads to another, and the two of you decide to save rent money by sharing an apartment. This progression leads many couples to the altar through a drift and growing expectation from friends and family. All too often these matches are doomed from the start because a huge must or must-not was overlooked.

But, you say, what is the harm of a fling with someone I have no intention of having a long-term relationship with? There is no harm if three conditions are met. First, she needs to understand that you have no long-term interest in her. Second, you have to be the kind of person who is able to resist the feminine wiles of an unsuitable mate, and, third, both of you have to recognize and accept that this relationship is occupying time that could be spent finding the love of your life.

All of the above assumes that you are ultimately seeking a long-term, high-quality love relationship with the man or woman of your dreams. If you are in a different place in your life and not presently interested in a long-term love relationship, then much of this book does not apply.

How to make a must/must-not list

The quality of the list is directly proportionate to the quality of your self-knowledge. What are your values? Do you value a certain religion? Do you value education? Do you value money? Do you value social status? How important are looks, height, weight, fitness, health, mental health, etc.?

Remember that the must/must-not list is a list of deal killers. If a must is not present or a must-not is present, you will not consider a serious relationship with the person. As suggested above, you might not want to even date the person to avoid the possibility of getting into a relationship that ultimately must be broken off.

If the bar is set too high, you will reduce the pool of potential candidates to zero. Too low, and you will have many years to regret not being more selective. Remember the effect of time in the house example. A willingness to wait increases the size of the pool of possible candidates, as long as you are doing things to get out and meet more and more people.

Musts and must-not's are all-or-nothing, nonnegotiable qualities. These would be things like must be able to read and write and must-not have a felony conviction for a violent crime.

A second list of wants or "nice to haves" will help you to narrow down the list of those who pass the must/must-not cut. Knowing the difference between a must and a want is incredibly important but difficult to achieve. Let's suppose you are a baseball fan and you want a partner who will watch every MLB game you can record on your DVR with you. You cannot imagine getting serious about someone who will not do this, nor imagine this person being happy with you being glued to the tube for endless hours of baseball if he or she is not a baseball nut too. Interest in watching lots of baseball in this case would be a must. Let's further suppose that this person is a Yankees fan and you are a Cardinals fan. Is loyalty to a certain team a must or a want? Only you can decide.

Your list is a direct reflection of you and what you care about most. You might require a nonsmoker who loves cats and dogs or a vegetarian who is good with kids. Knowing what you genuinely want requires you to dig around in your brain and ask yourself hard questions over and over until you have answers.

Note: At this point you might feel a little creepy about being analytical and methodical about something as emotional as love. Get over it! You need to engage your rational mind before irrational infatuation or lust leads you down a path to disaster.

Historically these decisions were coolly made for children by parents or a village matchmaker because the children were judged to not have the rational powers or life experience to do it for themselves. In our society, you have the freedom and the responsibility to make your own decisions. This decision is one of the most important you will make in your life. Get it right!

In my case I needed and still need a good person, good with kids, intelligent, not crazy (notice the precise psychological terminology), family oriented, fun loving, and adventurous. The want list includes things like cute, brunette, nice body, and loves good food. My bride is all of these and more.

Are you the man of her dreams?

When you finish building your list of musts/must-not's and wants, look at it and ask yourself, "Why would someone like that want anything to do with me?" Be careful with this question. Taken too far, you will find yourself slipping into Karen Horney's neuroses numbers 1 and 9. I'm talking about an honest self-appraisal. What do you have to offer the woman of your dreams that might make you the man of her dreams?

Note: This book is written from the perspective of a man, me, and how he loves a woman, my wife. It may or may not apply to other relationships. The literature on relationships says that these principles are universal. I suspect that many of the principles are the same regardless of gender, sexual preference, etc. I even suspect that the same principles apply to close, nonsexual friendships, but I do not have direct experience that allows me to speak with confidence on that subject.

To stay on point, I will focus on a man loving a woman. Feel free to apply what you read to any relationship you wish. Please let us know your experience applying the lessons in those other relationships.

OK, we are back to you again and a good look in the mirror. What do you have to offer? Are you a good person? Are you fun to be around? Are you thoughtful? Are you kind, thrifty, loyal, or in any other way a good Boy Scout? If she is smart—and you do want her to be smart, don't you?—she will pay attention to how you treat your mother and your sisters to get a sense of how you treat females in general. What would she see? Are you a good listener? Are you making the most of the looks god gave you with good grooming, staying fit, and dressing well?

If a woman is given the choice of two otherwise identical men, one making minimum wage and the other with a career that can provide a comfortable lifestyle, which way do you think she will go? Are you applying whatever gifts and talents you have to making a good living?

Many women in my experience appreciate a guy who has a range of useful skills, from handyman to chef, janitor, bartender, wine steward, and massage therapist.

What kind of shape are your social and interpersonal skills in? Women like good listeners and conversationalists. Can you discuss movies and books that a woman might have seen or read? Are you involved in any community or charitable work? Do you have any interesting hobbies or things you are studying like gardening or a new language, or do you spend your life playing video games and watching YouTube?

How do you act in adverse situations? Are you cranky? Do you have an explosive temper? Do you show kindness and understanding? Are you a bully or wimp? Can you be firm and respectful as you problem solve and negotiate?

Are you a generally positive and upbeat person, or are you a doom and gloom negativist? We will see later that many of these items are not only involved with attracting the love of your life but are also critical to the permanence of the relationship.

Creating a lasting relationship with the woman of your dreams entails the kind of self-development and improvement that will cause you to be the man of her dreams. Nothing is more painful than unrequited love, so get going on being all that you can be.

Being the guy she wants includes an appropriate level of self-love and self-respect, since you have to have something before you can give it away. Self-love and self-respect are different from narcissism. Narcissists are terrible at relationships because everything is about them. As with everything on Karen Horney's list, good things taken to excess become bad things.

Knowing your weaknesses or the things that make you difficult to get along with is also important. Some of these may be on her must-not list and therefore will be deal killers. Finding this out sooner rather than later is a good thing.

PART TWO

Finding the Love of Your Life

Once you are "Love-Ready," you need to get out into the world and find the partner of your dreams. In this part, we cover three love lessons involved with the discovery and selection process:

"Have a bias toward action— let's see something happen now. You can break that big plan into small steps and take the first step right away."

—Indira Gandhi

Love Lesson Four

Give Yourself a Chance

Now that you are clear about the man or woman of your dreams, you have to give yourself a chance of meeting him or her. Women talk about having to kiss a lot of frogs before they find a prince. The male equivalent of that can also be true. It is also possible that you will find the love of your life immediately. Life is funny that way.

I confess that I have very little dating experience and very little knowledge of how to meet women. This lesson therefore is drawn from research, interviews, and observing others.

Online matchmaking services are one possibility. Most online dating services get mixed reviews. Studies do show that many singles are using these services. One study calculated that twenty-five million people used dating services in one month in 2011, the most recent year for which I could find statistics. Other studies suggest that up to a quarter of new relationships are formed online. Reading reviews and advice for surviving the online experience are a good upfront investment of time and energy before proceeding.

The old-fashioned and tried and true approach is to find ways to mix with people who have the kinds of interests and values you do. For example, if you love dogs, go to a dog park regularly and talk to people there. If religion is important to you, get involved in the broadest circle of people who are doing things related to the religion of your choice. Do you have interests in art, photography, kayaking, biking, tennis, or whatever? Join groups, take classes, go on vacations, etc., involving your interests.

The idea is to have fun doing things you enjoy while meeting people with similar interests in an environment that allows you to interact and have fun without pressure. The worst case is you will get out and have fun. You could even do some self-improvement by taking a cooking class, a wine appreciation class, a massage class, a yoga class, etc., to broaden your skills as well as your circle of acquaintances.

If you are shy or have difficulty meeting people, you will have to push yourself outside of your comfort zone and broaden your repertoire. Use every occasion to improve your abilities. Above all else, be yourself. Do not play a role. False advertising is a bad idea. If feelings of inadequacy are keeping you back, revisit the list of neuroses. Get counseling or life coaching if needed to get over this barrier.

There is a difference between "needing" someone in your life and wanting someone to share your life with. If you are too needy, you will act in ways that are counterproductive. Relax, meet people, and take an interest in them. There also is a problem with trying too hard and conducting the search for the love of your life as if it were the CIA's search for Bin Laden.

The key to success at this stage is to be armed with enough self-knowledge that you will recognize your true love when you meet. In order to meet this person of your dreams, you will need to spend time in situations likely to attract him or her, and you will have to continuously improve yourself so that when the two of you meet, magic can happen.

Once these preconditions are met, get on with enjoying your life.

The more you know about each person you meet, the more you will be able to determine their fit with your musts and wants. This is accomplished by being genuinely interested in them, asking good questions, and being a good listener. These are all skills that are essential in all aspects of work and life, so learn them and practice them.

Occasionally keep track of who is consuming the most "air time" in a conversation. Strive for more than half to be the other person's. If you are not sufficiently interested in someone to ask questions and listen carefully to his or her answers, there is a chance you are a narcissist or he or she is not the man or woman for you.

Where things go from here has everything to do with what you want. I am going with the assumption you want to find and bond with the love of your life. The rest of this book will be based on that assumption.

Depending on where you are in your life, many other goals may be more suitable. Maybe you are perfectly happy being single and want to have someone in your life who is also happy being single but who will enjoy a movie, dinner, or whatever with you from time to time. It all comes back to self-knowledge and knowing what is right for you at each phase of your life.

*When I eventually
met Mr. Right, I had
no idea that his first
name was Always.*

—Rita Rudner

Love Lesson Five

Decide Who is Out

The dating process is a time of discovery. Your previously prepared must/must-not and want lists will not tell you who the love of your life is, but they will tell you who he or she is not.

If you find yourself attracted to someone who is missing a must or has a must-not and you are still attracted to this person, one of two things is true. First, and most likely, you are allowing your emotions, a cute face, or a sexy butt to overwhelm your rational mind. Or maybe your must/must-not list is not a true reflection of what you need to be happy. This dilemma could lead you to a common mistake many people make, which is trying to fix someone.

You are not buying a house that can be renovated and upgraded. You are beginning a long-term relationship with a person. The deal killer you set aside in the heat of the initial romance is likely to come back to haunt you when the heat drops to a simmer.

Let's also remember that there are two people in this relationship. If the relationship is going to last, you have to be the man or woman of his or her dreams also. Help the other person to be very clear about what he or she needs and make an honest assessment of whether or not you are that man or woman.

For example, let's say that you have met an intelligent, warm, and sensitive woman. She is fun and has a great sense of humor, and she is a well-paid professional. She has used her considerable income to buy a beautiful ranch where she raises horses. Prior to meeting you, her horses were the love of her life, and on any given day she could prefer them to you.

Let's suppose that you think horses are stupid and that you despise flies and the smell of manure, and the last thing you want to do in your spare time is to be around horses. You are a man of the sea, and your preferred leisure activity is boating. Ideally you would like to take extended boating vacations.

The two of you could have incredible dates and even amazing short vacations (she can't be away from the horses for very long). You could fall in love and be crazy about each other. Could she learn to live without horses, or could you learn to live with them? It is possible, but it's not the way to bet.

The key here is to find the deal breakers early and to move on. The alternative is to postpone the inevitable and make the ultimate breakup more painful. Caveat: Seinfeld got a lot of comic mileage out of fixating on some small detail of an otherwise amazing woman and using that small detail as a deal breaker that ended the relationship. After nine seasons and 180 episodes in which he dated a vast array of women, his character was still single.

The decision to persist or to end the relationship and move on is never easy. It is also never possible to know for sure if you have made the right decision. If you are insecure, you could fear that you will never succeed in love.

I have often heard women say that all the good guys are married or gay so there is nothing left but jerks and losers. We know several women who married later in life or remarried later in life to wonderful men with whom they are happy today, so we know it is possible, even if it is challenging.

"So, I love you because the entire universe conspired to help me find you."

—Paulo Coelho

Love Lesson Six

And The Winner Is?

Let's assume that you have gotten out into the world and have met many people, most of whom are not a match for you. Let's also assume that you have now met several who have all of the musts, none of the must-not's, and several, but perhaps not all, of the wants. Let's assume further that you are pretty sure you are a good match for each of these wonderful candidates. How do you know which is "the one"?

Up until now I have been pushing you to use your brain to make decisions. It is finally time for your heart to take over. If all of the above assumptions are true, you probably could live happily ever after with any one of these wonderful choices. It is also true that any of these relationships could end badly. The process so far has been aimed at eliminating the most obvious relationship killers. Over time people change, and the day may come in any relationship when your partner outgrows you or vice versa. We will cover ways to minimize these risks and to maximize relationship bliss in later lessons.

Any attempt to forecast the future is error prone. Three kinds of errors are possible. The first is a false negative, which in this context would be excluding a person who could have been the absolutely best match for you. The second error is a false positive, meaning pursuing a relationship with someone who proves to be a poor match. The third error is not making a decision and losing opportunities because others get frustrated with your indecision.

To make the final decision, you will need to think, meditate, pray, or whatever else you do to allow your heart and mind to cross the line in major life decisions. After you have given your rational mind the opportunity to save you from foolishness, trust your heart. Down deep you know who the right person is. Take a leap of faith and dive in and begin to build a loving relationship.

PART THREE

Understanding Love

It is always a good idea to clarify a few terms before going too far into a topic. In this part we will cover two love lessons:

"To find someone who will love you for no reason, and to shower that person with reasons, that is the ultimate happiness

−Robert Brault

Love Lesson Seven

Love is Something You Create

Love

An intense feeling of deep affection

A deep romantic or sexual attachment to someone

—*Oxford Dictionary of the English Language American Edition*

The *Oxford Dictionary* is great as far as it goes. The problem with the definition is that it could apply to a neurotic relationship or a healthy one, and it could apply to a brief experience or a lifelong one. It also could be a one-way relationship, with one person "in love" and the other not.

Here is our definition of love, which is a little different.

Our Definition of Love

A lasting, healthy, and positive intense feeling of mutual deep affection, respect, admiration, romance, and sexual attraction between two people that is continuously renewed and deepened.

You will notice that in both definitions, love is a feeling. In our definition, love is a feeling that the two of you share.

You will also notice that in our definition, love occurs and improves over time. This means that it happens in the context of a relationship.

Relationships occur for the purpose of meeting human needs through another person. If one human could meet all of his or her needs without contact with other people, that human might not enter into relationships.

We do have needs, lots of them. Many of these needs can only be met through relationships. Others can be met outside of relationships, but they are more easily or successfully met through relationships.

Many theorists have attempted to develop models for understanding human needs. One of the most popular and widely known is Abraham Maslow. Maslow placed human needs in a hierarchy.

Maslow started with the most basic physiological needs that must be met to survive. Things like air, food, and water. These needs form the base of a pyramid.

The next layer of the pyramid is occupied by the needs associated with safety and security. Notice that if someone is sufficiently hungry or

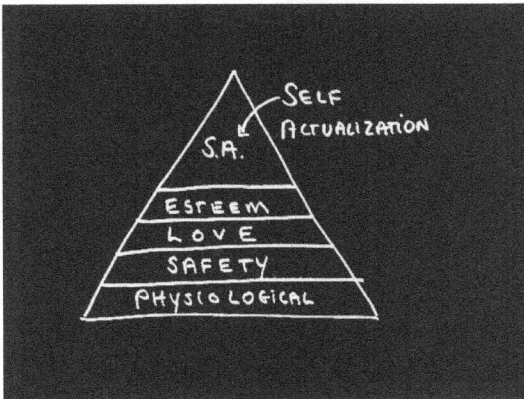

thirsty, he or she will take risks in order to satisfy that hunger or thirst. The more fundamental physiological needs trump the need for safety in this case. This demonstrates how unmet lower-order needs will override higher-order needs when unmet.

The next rung of the pyramid contains love and belongingness needs.

Love needs are followed by esteem needs. These needs have to do with prestige and a feeling of accomplishment.

The highest need is the need for self-actualization. This need is met by achieving one's full potential, often through some creative pursuit.

There are three key points to take away from Maslow's hierarchy:

1. The higher-order needs do not emerge until the lower-order needs are addressed. For example, it is hard to develop a romance with someone whose most fundamental needs for safety and survival are unmet. It also means that romance goes out the window when someone is extremely thirsty, hungry, sleep-deprived, and afraid.

2. Relationships can exist for the purpose of fulfilling any or all needs. There are societies in which women are prohibited from working outside the home. These same women may be unable to own property and may themselves be considered property. These women may have a relationship with a man exclusively for the purpose of meeting their most basic survival needs.

   Meeting fundamental biological and safety needs may be part of any relationship between two people in any society. This is especially true when it comes to raising children. Two people can more easily provide for the basic needs of food, shelter, warmth, and security when children are involved. Throughout human history this has been a major function of marriage.

3. To "be all that you can be" requires your love needs to be met. You cannot attain the highest good as a human being with unmet love needs. I do not believe that Maslow ever spelled it out in this way, but the hierarchy clearly tells us that higher-order needs do not reach preeminence until lower-order needs are met. This says to me that to be fully human and to do our best work in life, we need to meet our love needs.

Incredibly strong relationships are formed when two people are instrumental in meeting each other's needs at every level of Maslow's hierarchy. When two people work together to provide food and shelter as well as safety and security for each other, and these two people are in love with each other and support each other's development and growth, including support of creative acts that allow for self-actualization, bonds are formed in each need category, and the collective bond becomes incredibly strong.

Maslow provides one of many theories of human needs. It is referenced here because it is one of the simplest and most widely known. The main point in this book is not Maslow's theory but the principle that relationships are based on mutual human need satisfaction. The greater the need satisfaction, the stronger the relationship. Since lasting love occurs in the context of a lasting relationship, meeting your partner's needs, of all kinds, to the greatest degree possible is important for relationship strength and longevity.

Understanding your partner's unique mix of needs and how he or she prefers to have them met is one of the keys to mutual need satisfaction.

Gary Chapman, in his book *The Five Love Languages,* describes five different ways of expressing and receiving love. They are:

1. Words of Affirmation
2. Quality Time
3. Receiving Gifts
4. Acts of Service
5. Physical Touch

Chapman's book gives us another way of understanding how to give love in a way that is meaningful. It turns out that different people have different preferences. If your way of communicating love is out of whack with your partner's preferred way of receiving it, you are at risk for "a failure to communicate" of Cool Hand Luke proportions.

Chapman's approach argues for the superiority of the platinum rule over the golden rule. The platinum rule states that we should do unto others as they need to be done unto, which may be different from the way we want to be done unto.

The purpose of all of this "doing unto" is to create mutual need satisfaction and to therefore create a strong and enduring context in which love can exist.

Our definition of love requires the existence of certain feelings in another human being. But we cannot create feelings in another person; we can only create conditions that favor the development of the intended feelings. The way you do this is through your behavior. What you say and do not say and what you do and refrain from doing can create an environment in your presence where love has a chance to blossom.

There are several key points to note here. First, your thoughts or feelings are not known to the other person until you say or do something. You could be watching a football game and all the while daydreaming about the wonderful woman in the next room reading a novel, but what does she see, hear, and feel?

Second, she has a lot of control over her reaction to anything you do or say. If she is disposed to have love blossom, she can water and feed it. If she is not, she can hit it with weed killer.

The third point is that your words and actions must be congruent. They must be a true reflection of your thoughts and feelings.

Congruence is a fifty-cent word that means everything is aligned or in agreement. If, for example, the person you love walks into a room, you are likely to immediately feel happy. Is your happiness reflected in your face? Are you smiling? Do you look at him or her admiringly? Do you say something positive? Do you do something positive? Any mismatch between your facial expression, tone of voice, words, and actions breaks down congruence.

Every person is unique. What will engender a lasting healthy and positive intense feeling of mutual deep affection, respect, admiration, romance, and sexual attraction between two people that is continuously renewed and deepened will be somewhat different for each unique human being.

Some human needs are universal. The type of therapy I underwent and was trained to perform is called transactional analysis (TA). In addition to being a type of therapy, it is also a personality theory that tells us a lot about what makes most humans tick.

The most fundamental psychological needs, according to TA, are the needs to structure time and get strokes. Strokes are units of recognition, and they can be positive or negative. TA says that any stroke is better than no stroke at all.

People generally prefer positive recognition, but they will take negative recognition over being ignored. According to Eric Berne, TA's founder, people structure time to get strokes (recognition).

He proposed six ways in which humans structure time:

1. Withdrawal: Entering into their own private world, where only internal fantasy strokes are available. See love lesson eleven about establishing a rhythm of togetherness.

2. Rituals: From the simple "hi there, how are you?" up to elaborate rituals like a wedding.

3. Pastimes: Discussing books, movies, TV shows, the news, politics, sports, cars, computers, or whatever two people are interested in.

4. Activities: Often these include group activities such as playing golf. Is it just a coincidence that in golf the score is kept in strokes? I think not!

5. Games and Rackets: This category is way too complex for the purposes of this book. Games and rackets as defined in transactional analysis are also most often destructive to relationships.

6. Intimacy: In a state of intimacy, strokes are freely given and spontaneous. There are no ulterior transactions or motivations. Intimacy in this context is psychological

intimacy, which may or may not accompany physical intimacy.

Four of these time structures actively contribute to the building of lasting loving relationships.

Rituals: Many rituals can be established in a relationship to provide a steady and dependable supply of small strokes. For example:

- Clinking glasses at the commencement of every meal with a small toast that has a loving message in it

- Good night kisses

- Morning hugs

- Holding hands while walking

Pastimes: Finding an assortment of topics you both enjoy discussing and keeping the material fresh is another source of strokes for both of you.

Activities: In lesson eleven we will cover one strategy for building your repertoire of shared activities. Activities you do together are another dimension to your stroke exchange.

Intimacy: In this context we are talking about psychological intimacy, which may or may not be associated with physical intimacy. Intimacy is a free exchange of recognition without an ulterior motive. Berne claimed that it was a rare thing to achieve. I think it does not need to be rare in a psychologically healthy couple who are in love.

Since intimacy is the most powerful, positive, and psychologically satisfying form of recognition possible, I think increasing its presence in a relationship is important. Daily application of the lessons in this book can help to maximize intimacy in your life.

The love lessons in this book are based on fundamental human needs that can be applied to most people with a little adjustment for personal differences. Which lessons to apply and how to apply them is up to you and your best guess about which will do you and your relationship the most good.

"For one human being to love another: that is perhaps the most difficult of all our tasks, the ultimate, the last test and proof, the work for which all other work is but preparation."

—Rainer Maria Rilke

Love Lesson Eight

Love is Simple, but It is Not Easy

You have to really want it. This is the reason having a "why" is so important. Without a strong enough "why," you will not be able to do the "what" required. Love requires commitment, and it requires lots of ongoing effort to learn to create, build, and maintain a deeply loving relationship. Some of you may take a look at the suggestions in this book and say no way. The lessons in this book are not for every man, nor are they right for every woman. I know they work extremely well for me and my bride. If you decide to embark on this journey, be prepared to do what it takes.

Getting really good at anything takes ten thousand hours of effort. Malcolm Gladwell makes this point using many powerful examples in his book *Outliers*. That is roughly five years of forty-hour work weeks. Loving another person is something few get to do for forty hours a week, so it will take longer, maybe a lifetime.

Other studies have shown that the difference between people who are mediocre at something and people who are exceptionally good is the amount of deliberate, focused practice they engage in. In particular their willingness to practice things that are hard, things that show their weaknesses. Geoff Colvin provides compelling proof of this in his book *Talent is Overrated*.

I would argue that loving someone is more complex than playing the violin or playing chess (two types of expertise that have been closely studied). Therefore it will take many years of focused practice to become truly proficient.

Dr. Angela Lee Duckworth has researched success in a wide range of disciplines, and she has determined that the single best predictor of success is something she calls "grit." She describes her research in a TED talk filmed in April 2013. Below is an excerpt from her talk. Watch the whole talk at TED.com.

"My research team and I went to West Point Military Academy. We tried to predict which cadets would stay in military training and which would drop out. We went to the National Spelling Bee and tried to predict which children would advance farthest in competition. We studied rookie teachers working in really tough neighborhoods, asking which teachers are still going to be here in teaching by the end of the school year, and of those, who will be the most effective at improving learning outcomes for their students? We partnered with private companies, asking, which of these salespeople is going to keep their jobs? And who's going to earn the most money? In all those very different contexts, one characteristic emerged

as a significant predictor of success. And it wasn't social intelligence. It wasn't good looks, physical health, and it wasn't I.Q. It was grit.

Grit is passion and perseverance for very long-term goals. Grit is having stamina. Grit is sticking with your future, day in, day out, not just for the week, not just for the month, but for years, and working really hard to make that future a reality. Grit is living life like it's a marathon, not a sprint."

Are you gritty enough to be a great lover? Are you prepared to "do the hard yards" to build your skills and learn about the most mysterious force in the universe? If you are, it will take time and effort. Sometimes you will be rewarded for your efforts, and sometimes you will be frustrated. The only way you can be utterly defeated is if you give up.

As long as you are in there striving, the game is not over, and there is no loser. If you are very clear about why you are doing this, and your "why" is powerful enough, you will hang in there until you succeed. For many people, this will mean a number of initially promising relationships that go nowhere and perhaps even a few serious relationships that end in a breakup.

The pain associated with the false starts and breakups can be horrible. So horrible, in fact, that many people give up on the process entirely. So love is only for those with lots of grit, determination, and the ability to bounce back after setbacks. The same grit and resilience needed to enter into a long-term love relationship will be called upon time and time again during the life of the relationship.

A love relationship can be compared to a boat in which the two lovers travel the seas of life. The stronger the boat is, the better able it is to carry the lovers through storms. A weak boat will break up and sink in the first gale. A strong boat will make it through typhoons. The strongest of boats will even survive running aground on rocks. When it is towed off the rocks, the boat may have deep scars, and it may take time for all needed repairs to be made, but it will continue to safely carry the couple on their life journey.

PART FOUR

Love Skills

Part one covered how to get "Love-Ready." Part two was about finding the love of your life. Part three provided a foundation of knowledge needed to understand what a loving relationship is and what is needed to build and maintain a loving relationship. This part will cover some key skills that will nurture and develop a love relationship. The love lessons covered are:

LL9. Listen, Listen, Listen

LL10. Build Trust and Confidence

LL11. Create the Right Rhythm of Togetherness

LL12. Associate with Nurturing People

LL13. Open a Love Bank

LL14. Keep Withdrawals to a Minimum

LL15. Get on the Same Page and Stay There

LL16. Vulnerability is the Price You Must Pay

*"The first
duty of
love is to
listen."*

—Paul Tillich

Love Lesson Nine

Listen, Listen, Listen

I was smitten very early in my relationship with my wife to be. I wanted desperately to earn and keep her love. The first thing my wife remembers that impressed her is that we talked for hours and that I was intensely interested in what she had to say. The second was I respected her intelligence. What I remember is being so head over heels infatuated with this magnificent woman that I would have carefully listened to every word if she were reading the phone book aloud.

In addition to my wife's anecdotal report, there is a boatload of research that proves conclusively that there is no more powerful relationship builder than showing interest through good listening. Listening is the number one way to affirm another person.

Listening well involves listening with your ears, eyes, and your heart. It is important to understand the words, tone, timing, facial expressions, gestures, postures, and a thousand other things that convey meaning. You even want to listen for what is not being said. When you are completely engaged in listening, there is no time for anything else. You are totally consumed in the moment, and there is no one and nothing other than the person you love and what he or she is communicating. When you are listening at this level, you are creating a powerful connection that allows for a flow of feelings and meanings between you that often go well beyond the words.

Listening is also key to learning about your love's likes, dislikes, interests, desires, dreams, and fears. You want to know the turn-ons and turnoffs. Knowing what repulses and disgusts him or her can help you to avoid a situation that might be difficult to recover from.

One of my missions in life has been to become the world's greatest expert on my wife. This is not a chore, because I find her endlessly fascinating. I learn about her by asking questions, listening, reminiscing together about major events in our lives before we met, comparing childhood experiences, and just talking about the day.

We also frequently take time after a meal, vacation, or any other experience to evaluate it. One question we frequently ask is, "Is there anything we would do differently the next time?" This question is wonderful because it focuses on a positive future instead of criticizing the past. The past cannot be changed, but the future can. This question for us has established a continuous improvement cycle so that our enjoyment continues to spiral upward.

Through this question I have learned the fine points of how she likes each type of egg prepared among a thousand other preference details. For example, I know the type of movie she likes so well that I can do a better job than Netflix of predicting which movie she will enjoy.

Becoming an expert on your partner is not a once and done proposition. Your partner changes all the time. There are seasonal and daily mood changes, but there are also long-term changes that happen in a lifelong relationship. Paying attention, asking good questions, listening, and caring is a day in, day out relationship essential that will allow you to become the world's greatest expert on your beloved.

Great listening also requires undivided attention. This means no television, iPad, texting, or any other distraction during the conversation. Far too often multitasking results in several things being done poorly and none being done well. (Before you conclude this is just the ranting of some grumpy Luddite who is going to chase you off the lawn, go to a restaurant and watch couples who are on one screen or another during the meal and then notice the couples gazing into each other's eyes and holding hands. Which do you want to be?) Listening with every sense and your heart takes everything you have. If you are truly listening on every level, you will be in the moment and will not be prone to distraction or even the desire to speak. Few people listen at this level, and that is sad, because great listening enriches the life of the listener and the speaker.

Great listening often requires the use of good questions or prompts. Good questions are open ended and allow the speaker to go where he or she wants to go with the answer. Prompts stimulate the speaker to go on and to go deeper on topics.

Being heard feels good to the other person. Truly hearing provides insights about your love's needs, wants, desires, feelings, fears, and dreams that will allow you to apply the platinum rule covered earlier. If you take no other lesson in this book to heart, try this one, and you will be amazed, and your partner will be pleased by the result.

"Being deeply loved by someone gives you strength, while loving someone deeply gives you courage."

—Lao Tzu

Love Lesson Ten

Build Trust and Confidence

The willingness of a person to open up to you and share his or her desires, fears, etc., depends heavily on trust and confidence. Your partner must know that you will do no harm with the information obtained. Trust must be earned one small step at a time, and it can be lost in a heartbeat. In a flash of anger it is very tempting to use a tidbit you know to lash out at your partner. If you ever do, you will set the relationship back a mile. Trust and confidence also have a lot to do with the alignment of your words and your actions. It is vital that you say what you mean and mean what you say.

Trust and confidence mean you will have to open up too. Self-disclosure is a two-way street. Opening up and sharing your inner thoughts and feelings helps your partner to know how to better love you. Remember that our definition of love is not one way. While the focus of this book is on what the man needs to do to love a woman, almost everything applies to what a woman must do to love a man.

Your partner's level of trust in you will be based on all of your words and actions with every person you encounter. If you are hateful and vindictive with anyone, why should your partner believe that one day you will not be that way with him or her? If by contrast you are observed as being kind and thoughtful with everyone you meet, your partner can relax a bit more with you and feel safe.

Trust also comes from saying what you mean and meaning what you say. Kouzes and Posner, in their book *Credibility*, recount the research that shows the importance of alignment between your words and actions. They summarize this point with the acronym DWYSYWD—"Do What You Say You Will Do." Living by this rule means keeping your words and your actions aligned.

Saying "I love you" must be accompanied by a range of behaviors that demonstrate love for the words to be credible. Say it, and then back it up with behavior. Behavior says much more than words, and it says it more powerfully. Strive for ten behaviors that say I love you for every time you say the words "I love you." Use the words often, and look for a thousand ways to back the words up with behavior.

Trust and confidence are also built by recovering well from behaving badly. Since we are all human, we will sooner or later say or do something that reduces our partner's sense of trust, confidence, and safety. Showing genuine remorse and doing everything necessary to repair whatever damage has been done and then ensuring that there is not a repeat all go toward developing confidence that the relationship can survive some adversity.

It is important to remember that you cannot talk your way out of a problem that you behaved your way into. As with saying I love you in words and deeds above, any breach will have to be repaired with behavior.

A breach of trust is one of the things that some relationships will not survive. This of course depends on the severity of the breach and the strength of the relationship. Treat the trust and confidence placed in you as a most precious commodity to be safeguarded at all times. Sadly, far too many people squander the trust they are given and then have a lifetime to regret the relationship they destroyed.

"Let there be spaces in your togetherness, and let the winds of the heavens dance between you. Love one another but make not a bond of love: Let it rather be a moving sea between the shores of your souls."

—Kahlil Gibran

Love Lesson Eleven

Create the Right Rhythm of Togetherness

Time together and time apart are both important. The quantity of each is something the two of you will need to experiment with and talk about. My wife and I took off on our boat for eighteen months and were pretty much in sight of each other for the whole time. We would go to different parts of the boat to read and write from time to time, but mostly it was nonstop togetherness. Some couples would get homicidal under similar circumstances. Without the space constraints of the boat, we find that we enjoy some time apart to have experiences that we share when we are together. Each couple needs to find their own ideal rhythm and then get creative about making it work.

The first challenge you will have is finding time for the relationship. Everyone I encounter talks about not having enough time. Since this is not a book about time management, I will not attempt a comprehensive treatment of the subject, but I will reiterate a few key concepts and show how to apply them to a love relationship.

The first point about time is that you have all there is. You have twenty-four hours a day, and I have twenty-four hours a day. We cannot get more or use any less in a day. What differentiates people is what they do with their twenty-four hours. The most successful people allocate their time to the things that are most important to them. If your relationship is important, you will find time for it.

One of the best books on the subject is Stephen Covey's *The Seven Habits of Highly Successful People*, which is much more than a time management book and in my opinion is a must-read for all couples. Covey uses the example of trying to fit an assortment of rocks and sand into a container. If the container is filled with sand first, few rocks will fit, but if the container is first filled with large rocks, then small ones, and then sand, much more fits. When it comes to your time container, the big rock to put in first is relationship time. Note: Search for "Seven Big Rocks, Stephen Covey" on YouTube for a powerful visual demonstration of this principle.

We have gotten feedback from several couples about the power of creating a block of one-on-one time on a regular schedule. For us this means a daily evening discussion. Even when we are separated, we strive to have at least a brief conversation each evening. We use FaceTime and Skype to make video calls to each other even when we are in different countries. One loving couple we have discussed this with calls it "porch time." They have comfortable seating on their front porch, and they use that spot for their nightly talks. Give some thought to how you can build some "porch time" into your relationship. Make it one of the big rocks that gets into the jar first, and see what happens.

One time eater that can divide couples is their choice of recreational activity. We met that challenge early in our relationship. First we each made a list of all the recreational things we enjoyed. We are both active people with wide-ranging interests, so the lists were long.

Next we discussed items that were on her list but not on mine and vice versa. We decided to eliminate most of the things that did not appear on both lists. We took the list we had in common and added new "us" activities to it. For example, when our youngest started playing tennis on her school team, we went to a tennis camp and both became avid tennis players. The list has grown over the years to include many things we do together so that in the limited time available for recreation neither of us is sitting home waiting for the other.

Planning ahead and blocking time and then defending it is another tactic. This can be done weekly for "dates," and it can be done with a longer planning horizon for vacations. We will often book and pay for a vacation months ahead so that there is close to zero chance that we will let anything keep us from taking it.

If a relationship is important to you, you will need to invest time in it on a regular basis. Spending time with your beloved is a source of pleasure and joy, so it should be no hardship to forego something else in order to make time for him or her even if that something else is sleep.

*"The other night
I ate at a real
nice family
restaurant.
Every table had
an argument
going."*

—George Carlin

Love Lesson Twelve

Associate with Nurturing People

Friends and relatives can either enhance or detract from a relationship. Early in our relationship, my wife and I realized that after an evening with some other couples, we were irritable and treated one another in ways we did not like. After talking this through, we discovered that there are "toxic" friends and relatives. Toxic couples typically are not loving toward each other, and they bicker and say unkind things about their partners. We made an early decision to exclude toxic people from our life.

Our friends are all loving couples who have found their own special harmony that they bring with them to social occasions. This is not to say that they never argue or are never in a bad mood.

You and your love can be a source of inspiration to others, and you can uplift relationships by your example, but you must be careful to keep your dose of toxic contact to a manageable level.

Think of toxic people in the same way you think about other toxins like air pollution, for example. In a smog alert, the people at the greatest risk are people with heart and lung problems. If your relationship is a little rocky at the moment, you will need to keep toxic people contact to an absolute minimum. On the other hand, if your relationship is strong and some of the toxic people are close relatives, you can probably weather family gatherings without much adverse effect.

The key is awareness and monitoring the effect to manage it successfully.

"To give pleasure to a single heart by a single act is better than a thousand heads bowing in prayer."

—Mahatma Gandhi

Love Lesson Thirteen

Open a Love Bank

If you want to prosper financially, you need a savings and investment program that you contribute to regularly and that you withdraw from infrequently. Many people fail to do this because saving and investing involves a delay of gratification since the money you save and invest is enjoyed at some point in the future.

A "love bank" also requires regular deposits both large and small and infrequent withdrawals, but it does not involve a delay or gratification. In fact, the gratification is immediate, and it compounds in several ways. The first source of enjoyment is the mere act of giving love to someone else. The second source of immediate gratification is seeing the enjoyment the other person gets from the love you invest. Finally, the recipient is more disposed to give love back for a third immediate source of enjoyment.

In addition to the immediate benefits, there are long-term benefits. Everything you put into the love relationship builds it, makes it stronger, and helps the two of you to achieve ever greater depths of love.

Like a savings and investment plan, your "love bank" serves to build a reserve that can prevent the relationship from becoming bankrupt during lean times. As with its financial equivalent, it takes years of effort to build up an account, but it can all be lost due to one stupid move.

Deposits to the love bank are anything you do that builds the love relationship. Remember our definition of love.

> *A lasting healthy and positive intense feeling of mutual deep affection, respect, admiration, romance, and sexual attraction between two people that is continuously renewed and deepened.*

Using this definition, anything you do that creates intense feelings of affection, respect, admiration, romance, and sexual attraction is a deposit. Anything you do to decrease any or all of these things is a withdrawal.

One way of looking at this is to consider all of the things you could do to create an association in your lover's mind between you and all of the positive emotions listed in our definition.

To understand this, you need to look no further than the most basic introductory course in psychology.

What we are talking about here is classical Pavlovian conditioning. If you remember your lesson on Pavlov, it probably had something to do with bells and saliva. The take away lesson is that once an association is formed in the mind, as with the bell and the presence of food, the bell can initiate a physical reaction, which in Pavlov's experiments was salivation.

Think about this for a second. A ringing bell created a physiological change in the dog! I have seen and experienced numerous examples of Pavlov's classical conditioning in humans.

I once worked with a woman who had gone through a particularly nasty divorce. Her smart phone had a special ring tone for her ex. When the phone would ring with his ring tone, the physical transformation she underwent was obvious and profound. Her face contorted, her shoulders tensed, and she grabbed her stomach with one hand. If she were in a laboratory, I am sure it would be possible to measure changes in her brain activity, hormones, heart rate, skin conductivity, etc. All from a ring tone.

The opposite of this also occurs. When we love someone, we carry pictures of them with us because a glimpse of their face in a picture makes us feel good. When we are away, we call them on the phone to hear their voice, and that, too, makes us feel good. In a love relationship, our brain creates powerful associations between the person we love and all of the positive emotions listed in our love definition.

Go to any airport and watch people reuniting with someone they love. There is an obvious and significant transformation of the entire body when one lover sees, hugs, and kisses the other. Notice that the change is triggered by the fact that these people are seeing, hearing, smelling, and feeling each other. This is because deep in their minds there is an equal sign between a long list of positive emotions and all of the visual, auditory, olfactory, and tactical cues the lovers produce.

Thinking about Pavlov and dogs in connection with a love relationship can trigger concerns about manipulation, and the whole thing can seem devious on some level. There are a few key points to keep in mind regarding using these skills in devious ways.

First, if your motives are pure and you are striving to love another person better, you are not being devious. Second, we are manipulating one another all the time. The question is are we doing it well or not and are we doing it with positive intent or not. Third, classical conditioning exists like gravity. It is there all the time. We are constantly "reinforcing" people whether we know it or not.

Given these points, doesn't it make sense to positively reinforce the other person so that whenever that person sees you or hears your voice, he or she feels positive feelings and wants more?

This applies to all relationships, not just love relationships. If you can think of someone whose presence makes you feel good, chances are that person is routinely using the love skills outlined in this part. If, for example, someone shows genuine interest in you and listens carefully and thoroughly to you, it is likely you will associate him or her with positive feelings after only a few minutes.

I hope that after thinking about it for a while, you conclude that this whole Pavlovian conditioning thing is real and that, like gravity, ignoring it can lead to a painful fall. Once you reach this conclusion, it is only natural to start thinking about how to make it work for you and not against you.

If you have already started to become the world's greatest expert on the person you love, you will have a treasure trove of information about what that person does and does not enjoy. Use this information to maximize your beloved's pleasure and minimize his or her pain.

I know that in my marriage it is important for me to have routine things I do that demonstrate my love as well as little surprises that create delight. I suspect many men and women would enjoy this combination as well. Since you are the greatest expert on your beloved, you either already know or will soon find out the answer to what combination of words and actions will create a continuous stream of positive emotions and feelings in his or her association with you.

Actions speak louder than words, so constantly do things that support your words. Remember that what is pleasant or unpleasant may change by the hour, day, month, or year. This means that you will always need to listen, observe, ask good questions, and try new things if you are going to build, maintain, and deepen the feelings of love between you.

Common Sources of Positive Feelings

Food

I have yet to encounter a man or woman who does not like good food. Some are more hard-core foodies than others, but even "nonfoodies" enjoy a good meal. Cooking is one skill set everyone, male or female, should have. Preparing wonderful meals for your beloved is something that can be done often. Lovingly prepared meals are a way of taking a biological necessity and turning it into a delightful act of love.

Something as simple as making coffee in the morning can be an act of giving and receiving love.

Planning a meal, shopping for the ingredients, cooking, serving, and cleaning up is something both partners can do for each other as an ongoing way of demonstrating love to each other. Knowing your beloved's favorite foods and knowing precisely how he or she likes them prepared and learning the skill necessary to deliver those favorites is a way of taking this concept to a new level.

Stop at the store and pick up her favorite wine and dark chocolate for no particular reason as a way of providing a fun, inexpensive surprise.

Massage

A massage has numerous benefits, from easing sore muscles to creating deep relaxation. A massage is also a sensuous experience for both parties filled with delightful scents, sights, and sensations.

The best massages are done in a state of mindfulness, completely in the here and now with attention to the minutest detail. If the person giving the massage is completely tuned in, he or she can detect tension in tiny muscles and then work those muscles until the tension melts.

Massage is both an art and a science that needs to be studied and practiced. Aromatherapy, hot stones, shiatsu, and Swedish massage are just a few types of massage that can be learned. Each style and technique has its merits. Which one is right for you both? You will need to add that answer to your encyclopedic knowledge about your partner. Learning the art and science of massage also maximizes the efficacy and safety of a massage. A sports massage done after a particularly grueling workout or competition can speed recovery and healing while easing some discomfort.

The tremendous number of nerves in the feet makes a simple foot massage a great treat.

Laughter

Couples in love laugh together often. Laughter is a simple but exquisite pleasure that is good for our bodies and our souls. We know one wonderful woman who married the love of her life in large measure because when they were dating, he always made her laugh. Many years later they still enjoy a wonderful marriage, and he still makes her laugh. When two people are in love and comfortable with each other, it is possible to laugh at ourselves, the other person, or just about any of the absurdities of life.

Courtesy, Kindness, and Respect

Sadly, common courtesy is not very common. Why would you ever stop saying please and thank you to a person you love? In the case of a female partner, why would you stop holding the door for her? (OK, there are some women who find this offensive because it implies they are too physically weak to deal with the door themselves. If your love falls into this camp, let her open her own door.) For us, courtesy and kindness are a way of showing respect to each other and avoiding the impression that the other person is being taken for granted.

Every person has his or her own personal list of do and don't behaviors that convey respect, courtesy, and kindness. These can be little everyday things like clearing the table after a meal or putting down the toilet seat or waiting for the other person before starting to eat. Knowing your partner's list of dos and don'ts and sharing yours can help in establishing house rules.

Saying thank you is a way of reinforcing things that you like and making them happen more often in the future. It is also a way of recognizing some thoughtful act and giving genuine gratitude for it.

Small courtesies like offering to get a glass of water for your partner when you are getting one for yourself should be automatic.

The division of labor in your house is a matter of personal preference and negotiation. One courtesy you can do for each other is to try to make the other person's task as easy as possible. For example, if you do not wash the dishes, the least you can do is to rinse food off your plate before it hardens. If you do not mop floors, you can clean up spills as they happen. If you do not do laundry, you can ensure all dirty laundry is in the clothes hamper and not strewn about.

Compliments

When you feel something positive, such as the enjoyment of looking at your partner, share that feeling by telling him or her. If you say things like this often, find new ways of expressing yourself to keep it fresh. Loving couples are each other's most enthusiastic cheerleaders. Applauding a good shot on the tennis court or the golf course or a well-played hand of cards is simply a way of conveying your admiration for the person of your dreams.

Focus on the Positive

This famous picture is used to illustrate some

key points about perception. When you look at the picture, do you see a young woman or an old woman? Whichever you see, look for the other. They are both there. If you continue to see one but not the other, enlist some help from someone else. Eventually you will be able to see both. The one that jumps out at you is called "figure," and the one that disappears is called "ground."

Figure and ground are part of everyday life. There is infinitely more to perceive than we can handle, so we have to focus on some subset of reality. You can choose to do this with someone you love. You can focus on the positives and let everything else become ground. Just as with the picture, once you see both the old woman and the young one, you know both are there, but you can choose to focus on one of them.

When I look at my wife, I see the young woman. She describes this phenomenon as me having my "love blinders" on. Focusing on a loved one's positives does not mean that you do not see the rest of the picture. It just means you choose to focus on the best part of the picture. This tends to be more enjoyable for both of you.

I have encountered some women who believe that compliments from a man are a way of exercising control over women and that the compliment giver is setting himself up as judge and jury and therefore is placing himself in a dominant status. I am not married to such a woman, and therefore I will express my delight in her to her on all possible occasions.

Play

When you play together with your partner, you are not necessarily the source of pleasure, but you are present and sharing the pleasure with him or her. These shared pleasurable events also serve to reinforce the relationship. If the two of you go to a concert or a movie and have a good time, the good feelings are associated with the relationship.

We also find that anything that we might enjoy separately we will likely enjoy even more together. Building in play time and having a large repertoire of play activities you can enjoy together is one way of nurturing the relationship.

Sometimes play involves competition. We have seen this become a problem for lovers when neither can stand to lose. Fortunately for us, I do not mind losing.

Being Best Friends

According to the *Merriam Webster Dictionary*, a friend is a person you like to be with. A best friend, therefore, is the person you like to be with the most. My wife is my best friend. When we are in our "friend" mode, we do all of the things good friends do. This includes working on projects around the house, discussing the books we are reading or the movie we just watched, or just "hanging out" together. My wife plays many roles in our life. She is my girlfriend, my lover, my playmate, my partner, and my best friend. Each of these roles, along with the roles she plays with other people, such as mom, aunt, sister, cousin, etc., brings something special to our relationship.

Sex

I bet you thought I would never get to the juicy part. Sex is a gift to couples from Mother Nature. It is as though Mother Nature said, "I'm going to give the two of you some really hard stuff to do, but to balance things out I'm going to throw in a really fun thing too." At the most basic level, sex provides pleasurable sensations and possibly children. At its best it is a spiritual union that transports two people to a new level.

When looked at scientifically, sex produces a psychobiological cascade of hormones beginning with testosterone and estrogen. These hormones are a major factor in libido, or lust.

The sex act itself produces large quantities of dopamine. Dopamine is central to the brain's pleasure/reward system that causes us to want to repeat the act. Dopamine even alters the way we remember and causes us to bond to one partner. Women produce the hormone oxytocin, the substance in the brain that creates attachment. It is a major player in the bond between mother and infant when they are physically close, and it is the "cuddle" hormone produced when a couple are close after sex.

Men produce vasopressin, which is also referred to as the "monogamy hormone," and it has the same effect as oxytocin has on a woman. It bonds a man to a woman.

This entire chemistry set is in place to ensure that we are attracted to one another and to ensure that we bond to each other so that we reproduce and so that infants with no way to survive on their own have the resources they need.

All of the above is not only important to the survival of the species, it is also important to the survival of a loving relationship. A healthy sex life is one of the forces we can harness to maximize the bond we have.

The key with sex, as with all other things in a relationship, is to understand the needs, desires, preferences, turn-ons, and turnoffs of your partner and then to do the things that please him or her and refrain from the things that do not. It is also important to be able to share your own desires, preferences, etc.

As with everything else in a relationship, you can learn a lot about your partner by being observant, asking good questions, and listening to the answers. Many people find talking about sex awkward. For the conversation to go well, a high level of trust and comfort needs to exist. This is built outside the bedroom as described earlier in this book.

As with all other things, this is not a once and done process. It is a never-ending process as people's needs and desires change hour to hour, day to day, week to week, and over the years through all of the stages of life.

In most cases, the quality of your sex life is likely to parallel the overall quality of your love relationship.

"Of all the animals, man is the only one that is cruel. He is the only one that inflicts pain for the pleasure of doing it."

—Mark Twain

Love Lesson Fourteen

Keep Withdrawals to a Minimum

If we are striving for *"Intense feelings of mutual deep affection, respect, admiration, romance, and sexual attraction,* "we want to avoid doing anything that detracts from these feelings. The advice in this lesson suggests some things that commonly cause a reduction in these feelings. As with everything in this book, it is important to customize your actions to fit who you are and who the person you love is.

The fact that people seek pleasure and avoid pain is about as psych 101 as it gets. This point should be obvious. I find it astounding to watch a couple inflict insult and injury on one another and then expect to have a lasting positive relationship.

This does not mean that couples do not have energetic debates and discussions, nor does it mean that you cannot confront or push back in a relationship. Real relationships require all of the above. You have needs, preferences, and values that may at time be at odds with the person you love. The key is how you treat him or her as you deal with these issues.

Part of the conundrum is that tough love is love too, and sometimes being tough with the person we love is the most loving thing we can do.

The keys here are the frequency, the intent, and the delivery. If harshness is infrequent, done for a noble cause, and lovingly and carefully delivered, it probably is a plus and not a negative at all.

Things that put a dent in the love account

Criticism

Honest feedback is an essential part of a relationship. In many cases, a wife is the only person in the relationship who will tell her husband things that will prevent him from embarrassing himself in public.

Giving and receiving feedback can be a source of pain and a divisive force if it is not handled well

Couples who engage in nonstop criticism, especially in public, are driving a wedge into their relationship that it may not survive. Constructive criticism, by contrast, is a relationship builder. This point comes through loud and clear in the research conducted by Dr. John Gottman, who claims that he can identify couples that will divorce after watching them interact for as little as fifteen minutes. The predictor of divorce is not the fact that negative feedback is given but how it is given.

Constructive criticism must be delivered the right way, at the right time, and in the right place. Ideally it is delivered on request.

The right place is going to almost always be in private. Criticism is difficult enough to receive without the added problem of being humiliated in front of others. The right time is when both parties are relaxed and not in an agitated or defensive state.

The right way involves communicating love and respect in conjunction with the criticism. It is also important to not dwell on the past but rather focus on what needs to be different in the future. The past cannot be changed, and so there is little point to dwelling on it. The key is to learn from the past to do something in the present that will create a better future. This could even result in a plan to help one another when a similar situation emerges in the future.

Consider these two examples

Example One

You and your beloved are having dinner with another couple. She gets into a long-winded story, and you notice that the other couple have started to check e-mail on their smart phones and are looking at their watches and yawning. You could say, "Can you cut to the chase? You are boring everyone to tears," and then plan where you will sleep that night.

Example Two

You and your beloved are having dinner with another couple. She gets into a long-winded story, and you notice that the other couple have started to check e-mail on their smart phones and are looking at their watches and yawning. A minute or two later, your wife concludes the story, and the conversation shifts to someone else.

In the car on the way home, providing everyone is sober and in a good mood, you start a discussion about the evening. Ideally she says something like, "Did you have a good time?" to which you respond with whatever positives you genuinely feel, such as, "You look stunning tonight, the restaurant was great, and overall it was a fun evening. There was one point when you were telling the story about X when I thought you went a little long, and Mr. and Mrs. Y were checking out. In the future is there some kind of signal I can give you to let you know to cut it short?"

Example two may not be an easy conversation, but it stands a much better chance of success than example one. By the way, this example actually happened, but I was the long-winded one and my bride was the one confronting me constructively.

We now have a number of subtle and not so subtle cues she can use to tell me things in public.

One of the keys to criticism is to not sweat the small stuff. Focus on the positives, and let most of the negatives go. People are a package deal. We all have our flaws. Dwelling on them is rarely helpful.

What is helpful is to seek feedback from your partner when you are in a mental state to receive it. Feedback you seek is much easier to deal with than feedback that seeks you. If you seek feedback from her and she seeks feedback from you, the two of you can be powerful contributors to each other's continuous self-improvement.

Apathy

The opposite of love is not hate. It is apathy. Anything you do or fail to do that communicates apathy to you partner can inflict significant pain. Failing to notice things is a common problem for men, and the things she wants you to notice are up to her. Find out what they are and be sure to notice them. The list could include anything from new nail color, to the Nobel Prize on the mantle, furniture arrangement, or almost anything else.

Most importantly, never fail to notice your partner. When your partner enters a room, stop whatever you are doing and look at him or her.

When I do this, my bride often says, "I'm sorry to interrupt you," and to this I reply, "You are the main thing. Everything else is an interruption," and I mean it. Think about it for a minute. When the love of your life enters a room, what is more important?

"If you go to work on your goals, your goals will go to work on you. If you go to work on your plan, your plan will go to work on you. Whatever good things we build end up building us."

—Jim Rohn

Love Lesson Fifteen

Get On the Same Page and Stay There

Early in our relationship we started to take one vacation a year in a place that provided peace and solitude and not too many distractions. Lean years meant a Spartan location, prosperous years meant more comfortable surroundings. Both work well. We devised a strategy for these vacations that we found very powerful.

For each vacation, we purchase a notebook. On day one of the vacation, we take a long walk, usually on a beach, and we talk about what we liked about the last year. This review of the positives helps us to remember how much fun and love we enjoy together. Reviewing twelve months of these memories in a day creates something of an emotional high. At the end of the walk we return to our room and write out all the things that we like and then set the book aside and spend the day in play and relaxation.

On the second day of the vacation, we walk and talk about the things we did not like about the last year. We do this without criticism or rancor. We both try to hear and understand the things we each found unpleasant and why. As with day one, we return to the room, write down the things we did not like, and then enjoy the rest of the day.

On the third day, we talk about where we want our life to be in one, five, and ten years. By now you know the pattern: at the end of the walk we write the results of the conversation down and then play.

On the fourth day, we talk about ways to make the good things we discussed on day one happen more often, and we also talk about new positive things we would like to incorporate going forward.

On the fifth day, we talk about ways to reduce the frequency and severity of the negatives we captured on day two. The ideal, of course, is to totally eliminate the negatives.

On the sixth and seventh days, we plan how we will incorporate the ideas from the previous days into the next year so that we enjoy more positives, fewer negatives, and move our life to our one-year vision and a year closer to our five- and ten-year visions.

This process has been immensely powerful for us. The sequence of the dialog helps to keep it productive and open. Doing it in a place that is peaceful and free of distractions is a plus, but I'm sure it could be done on a series of Saturday mornings at home or in some other creative format that works for you and your life. The key is that we are on the same page, trying to attain the same things. We are attaining those things in a way that makes life better now and in the future, and we both have "skin in the game."

Because we create the plan together, we hold ourselves and one another accountable. If we get off track, we problem solve together. When we are successful, we celebrate together as co-creators of the success.

Where do you want to be one, five, ten years from now? Are there things you would like to see happen more often next year? Less often? What is stopping you from getting and staying on the same page with your partner in life?

"Love is giving someone the power to destroy you but trusting them not to."

—Unknown

Love Lesson Sixteen

Vulnerability is the Price You Must Pay

During a recent visit to the Getty in Los Angeles, I was captivated by a painting by Louis Jean Francois Lagrenée titled "Mars & Venus, Allegory of Peace."

Here is the museum's description of the painting.

> *"In this painting Mars, the Roman god of War, throws back the rich green bed curtains that frame the scene. As the drapery parts, the morning light spills in to reveal the form of the sleeping Venus, the Roman goddess of love. Mars gazes at her, utterly captivated by her beauty. Her love has tempered his fierce character, and his shield and sword lie abandoned on the floor. Echoing the lovers' bliss, a pair of white doves, symbolizing Peace, build a nest in Mars's helmet."*

Imagine that you and the person you want to love are wearing medieval suits of armor that you can never remove. What would the impact be on your ability to achieve an intimate relationship?

Many people go through life with the psychological equivalent of a suit of armor on at all times and wonder why they have difficulty attaining intimacy. Intimacy is a state that two people can achieve when their defenses are put aside and they allow themselves to be completely vulnerable in each other's presence.

Intimacy is scary stuff because without defenses you can get hurt. As a matter of fact, it is pretty much a sure bet you will be hurt. No one on earth can do the kind of damage to me that my wife can. A few unintentionally sharp words from her can cut deep while the same words from someone else would bounce off harmlessly.

I believe that it is impossible to attain the highest levels of love and intimacy without becoming defenseless and completely open to your beloved. This takes a leap of faith and deep trust in another person. The pain that will inevitably be experienced from time to time is more than offset by the joy of love experienced most of the time.

Dr. Brene Brown is a researcher, author, and lecturer who has studied vulnerability at length. Her TED talk on vulnerability (view it at TED.com) has been viewed 16.5 million times by people around the world. Below is a quote from her book Daring Greatly: How the Courage to Be Vulnerable Transforms the Way We Live, Love, Parent, and Lead.

"Vulnerability is the birthplace of love, belonging, joy, courage, empathy, and creativity. It is the source of hope, empathy, accountability, and authenticity. If we want greater clarity in our purpose or deeper and more meaningful spiritual lives, vulnerability is the path.

This vulnerability extends to the inevitable devastation that will be experienced by the partner who lives the longest. My wife and I were both blessed by having parents who were deeply in love. In both cases our fathers died first. My mother lived more than forty years longer but did not remarry because she said there was not another man on the planet who could ever measure up to the man she married. When my father-in-law died, my wife tried to comfort her mom by telling her it would be all right. Her mom replied that it would never be all right again, and it was not.

These two examples do not imply that someone who loses a great love to death will never love again. We have wonderful examples of people who, after a period of being devastated by their loss, were able to begin again and find true love.

What stops you from being vulnerable? How can you take steps today that will build toward a future relationship that is incredibly intimate because you have found a way to get rid of the armor and are ready to suffer the slings and arrows that love demands?

PART FIVE

Thorns in the Rose Garden

In this part we will deal with the topics that typically stress relationships and what you can do to manage them through these love lessons:

LL17.   Manage Conflict Constructively

LL18.   Tame the Green-Eyed Monster

LL19.   Deal with the Envy of Others

It is possible to find the love of your life, build a strong, loving relationship with him or her, and then to destroy the whole thing because the two of you mishandle issues that stress love relationships. The research on this topic is crystal clear.

The good news is that with a few bits of knowledge and a few skills, couples can dramatically improve their odds of preserving and even enhancing their relationship. When a relationship successfully comes through a tough challenge, both lovers have increased confidence that together they can face whatever may come next.

*"Peace is
not absence
of conflict, it
is the ability
to handle
conflict by
peaceful
means."*

—Ronald Reagan

Love Lesson Seventeen

Manage Conflict Constructively

From time to time, no matter how compatible the couple and no matter the love they enjoy, there will be conflict. You could even say that the relationship is not mature until it successfully makes it through a major conflict. The way a couple processes conflict is one of the most important predictors of their long-term success. Handling conflict constructively and respectfully tells the other party that no matter the issue, you can and will work it out.

Handling conflict badly is the single best predictor of divorce. Dr. John Gottman, a leading research scientist on marriage and family who was introduced to you back in love lesson fourteen, is the guy who can predict divorce with over 90 percent accuracy by watching a couple manage a conflict for just fifteen minutes. Dr. Gottman also claims that training high-risk couples to change a few conflict management behaviors can go a long way toward reducing the risk of a breakup. You can google John M. Gottman, PhD, and his coauthor on several publications, Nan Silver, for more information. I highly recommend his book *The Seven Principles for Making Marriage Work* for further reading.

Conflict Happens in a Context

The first thing to know about conflict is that it happens in the context of the relationship.

If you have applied previous lessons, you will have a positive context for conflict resolution:

By applying lessons 1–8, you have your own head screwed on straight, and you did the hard yards to become love-ready and find the partner of your dreams.

By applying lessons 9–16, you have opened up all channels of communication, gotten on the same page, created trust and confidence, shown your vulnerability, and bonded with your love by being a constant source of pleasure and a negligible source of pain. Your love bank should have a balance in it that will more than pay for any conflict you encounter, with lots to spare.

If you are doing all of this, what are the odds that the two of you will not have the ability to deal with a little conflict now and then? An ounce of prevention really is worth a pound of cure when it comes to conflict. The strong positive context built by the consistent application of the first sixteen love lessons makes dealing with the hard stuff so much easier than it otherwise would be.

Unfortunately, life is not as linear and neat as this. We are often into major conflict before we get anywhere near the ideal described above. The context for conflict often involves fatigue with or without sleep deprivation, financial stress, work stress, and family stress, and may also involve illness, hormonal fluctuations (in men and women), and a variety of other confounding factors.

The second thing to note is that severe conflict often erupts after numerous small injuries and insults are saved up and then cashed in in a spectacular fashion.

There are only three real options

There are three, and only three, constructive ways of dealing with conflict. They are:

1. Accept
2. Confront
3. Change the Situation

All conflict resolution will come from one of these three actions on your part. Unfortunately, there is no fourth option, so you have to choose one of the three.

Acceptance is the first line of defense. Since many things in the real world are just a fact of life, it is the one resolution strategy we will be called upon to use most often. We want to save the heavier-duty options for the handful of things that matter the most to us. Genuine acceptance involves moving an item from the bucket in our brain labeled "This bothers me" to the bucket in our brain labeled "No problem." Acceptance is a case of mind over matter. If you don't mind, it does not matter. The key here is not to deceive yourself into thinking you have accepted something when you have actually stuffed it down into a sack that when full will blow apart with catastrophic results. Anything stuffed down in the sack also burns away like an acid on the relationship.

"Stuffing it," therefore, is not a real option for anything other than the very short term while you get your head around how to fully and constructively process the conflict. Genuine acceptance redefines the event.

Let's suppose you are feeling "frisky," and you suggest an amorous evening to your lover. Let's suppose your lover is tired, not feeling particularly well, and is not in the mood. You could get upset, have your ego bruised, and behave badly, or you could tell yourself "The best loving is always when we are both in the same mood, so a delay is really best for both of us."

If you say something like this to yourself and really buy it, the conflict is over. If this is not working for you, there are two options remaining: confront and change the situation.

Option two, confront, does not mean attack. This type of confrontation is constructive. With each of these options there are fine points. There is a fine line between acceptance and stuffing it, and there is a fine line between constructive confrontation and hostile attack.

One of the keys in a love relationship is to remember who you are having this conflict with. If the other person is the love of your life, how are you going to treat him or her? I hope your answer is lovingly. Now that we know you are going to treat your partner lovingly no matter what, the question is what does lovingly look like when confronting?

Let's start with what it does not look like. Dr. Gottman, the guy who can predict divorce after watching a couple for fifteen minutes, says one of the flags he looks for in a doomed marriage is the "harsh startup." A harsh startup is characterized by sarcasm, strong criticism, or contempt.

Constructive confrontation is much more focused on a specific behavior and the effect it has on the person confronting. Dr. Thomas Gordon published *P.E.T. Parent Effectiveness Training* in 1970, and the information contained in it is just as valid today. Incidentally, P.E.T. concepts work in any human relationship, not just parents and children. Gordon's I-message, or I-statement, is one way of engaging someone assertively and confronting constructively.

Let's take a situation that I have heard some couples have experienced.

In the dark of night she gets out of bed, goes into the bathroom, and sits down, only to discover that the toilet seat has been left up. After a shockingly chilling dunk, here are a list of her possible reactions:

1. She decides on acceptance. After all, her husband hardly ever forgets to put the seat down. He is a great guy who treats her like a goddess and would never knowingly cause her to have an unpleasant experience.

2. She does not want to let it go and feels that she must confront, so after recovering sufficiently, she confronts by saying (he is already awake from the scream he heard), "You left the seat up, and I got a very unpleasant and dangerous surprise just now."

3. She is ripping mad and fed up with this guy, so she lashes out with, "You @#!%ing idiot! You left the !@# seat up again. What the @#ck is wrong with you?"

Which of the three reactions is going to peg Dr. Gottman's divorce prediction meter?

Reaction one would take superhuman forbearance and would have the downside of not informing the husband of the unpleasant and dangerous situation his actions caused and thus would not give him the benefit of useful feedback.

Reaction two is constructive confrontation, which in a loving relationship is going to result in an immediate apology. People who love each other do not want to be the cause of a toilet dunking. Notice that option two is an I-message that specifies the problem behavior and its effect.

Reaction three is the opening salvo in a battle that could lead to a war. It would take enormous maturity on his part not to get angry and defensive. Defensive reactions are often equally critical and contemptuous and the result in escalation of the conflict.

Changing the situation is the third legitimate way of handling conflict. Let's suppose that the toilet seat episode happens with some frequency and is the result of a nocturnal visit to the bathroom by him when he is half asleep. In this half-asleep condition, despite his best intentions, the seat remains up one out of ten times.

There are several ways to employ the "change the situation" option to this problem. If you have two bathrooms in the house, you could have a "his" and a "hers," or you could install an automatic toilet seat. Here is the description from Amazon:

Save your marriage OVERNIGHT by installing this sensor operated Touchless Toilet Seat. The lid cover will be lifted touch-

free when you approach, wave one more time on the sensor to lift toilet seat for men use; both lid and seat will close automatically 15 seconds after you walk away. No more falling into the toilet bowl or being lectured over coffee in the morning. So now you can keep your vows and your dignity till death do you part. - 100% touch-free, virtually eliminating the spread of germs - Occupancy Sensor range is easily adjusted, allowing the unit to be installed in a wide variety of bathroom shapes and sizes - Best Bang for Your Buck upgrade in your bathroom. Easy D.I.Y. installation - Perfect for people with disabilities, senior citizens, and families with children - The seat can be easily slid off for easy cleaning and is coated with anti-bacterial Silver Technology for added protection against germs - Comes with AC Power Adaptor - Round Model

I did not know such a product existed until I started working on this example. The manufacturer considers the product to be a marriage saver. Who knew?

Another way of changing the situation would be for her to check the seat each time before sitting down. If she is willing, and if she does not forget in the middle of the night, the problem is solved.

Notice that the resolution often begins with constructive confrontation, and this is followed by some sort of problem-solving process.

What appears to be conflict is often misunderstanding

Treating any conflict as a misunderstanding from the outset is beneficial no matter what the true nature of the conflict is. The way misunderstandings are cleared up is through the use of two skills covered earlier. These are good questions and good listening skills. It is also important to understand that managing interpersonal conflict through text messages, posts to Facebook or twitter, and even e-mail is not only likely to fail but also might deepen the misunderstanding and worsen the conflict. The phone is only marginally better than the other communication modes mentioned. Face to face is almost always the best.

In a situation that appears to be a conflict, special caution must be taken with questions. When people are frustrated or angry, they can easily "weaponize" questions. A question like, "What the hell is wrong with you?" is not an attempt to create dialog and understanding. It is an attack in question form. The highly skilled among us can use words that seem much more innocent but nuance them in a way that they cut like a knife. Use questions to open a dialog and create understanding only.

In approximately 80 percent of the cases, opening a dialog will resolve the misunderstanding, and the conflict will disappear. The remaining 20 percent of the cases will fall into one of the following categories:

1. Disagreement about Facts
2. Disagreement about a Decision
3. Values Conflict

Disagreements can be over the silliest things. The news is filled with tragic outcomes to silly disagreements. A woman in our little town is currently awaiting sentencing for murdering her brother because of a disagreement over chores. According to research I have reviewed and my own experience, the most common disagreements in couples have to do with children and money. These disagreements are often more substantive, and their resolution can have major consequences, so they must be handled well.

No matter what the topic, resolution will come in one of several ways. The first way is by agreeing to disagree. This is the simplest and easiest for disagreements that simply do not matter. The second way is by going to a source. Google and Siri resolve millions of disputes a day in this fashion. When we are only disagreeing about objective facts this works well.

The stickier disagreements are those where there is not a clear-cut answer but there are strong opinions. How strict or how lenient to be with children, for example, does not lend itself to a google search. The same could be said about how much money to spend versus save in any week. In these cases it is useful for the couple to spend a lot of time and effort up front agreeing to a set of principles and then to use those principles to guide their decisions. The whole life planning process described in love lesson fifteen establishes a foundation for these decisions.

Disagreements sometimes need to be negotiated. In any negotiation it is important to be principle focused and not position focused. Let's suppose there is a debate about where to go on the next vacation. The solution is easiest if both parties talk about the kind of experience they want to have and how much they want to spend and then look at all destinations that meet the established criteria instead of starting the conversation with one person saying we ought to go to destination X and the other saying destination Y. When we are principle focused, we can both win. When we are position focused, someone must lose. Fisher and Ury from the Harvard negotiation project wrote an entire book on this subject called *Getting to Yes*.

Values conflicts are the final type of conflict we encounter, and they are a special case because values are not negotiable. Ideally, major values clashes surface early in the relationship. Some of these can be deal breakers, so surfacing them early is important. For example, if religion is extremely important to one person but not at all to the other, it is possible to manage the practical issues, such as what the nonreligious person does while the religious person is attending church, synagogue, or mosque. The religious person might also feel strongly about raising children in the faith. If the nonreligious person has no objections, then this can be managed too. For some people, however, religion could turn into a holy war.

Other kinds of "religious" wars can erupt over which baseball or football team each partner prefers.

Conflict management is a learnable skill set. It is best to learn it before you need it so that you can build your skill to a high level before you use these skills to preserve the most important relationship in your life. If you are not highly skilled, getting help from a life coach, counselor, therapist, or other knowledgeable advisor can be extremely valuable.

In the hundreds of conflict management seminars I have given, I have interacted with thousands of participants about conflict at work and at home. Many of the one-on-one conversations I have had with participants were about conflict in their love relationships. My observation about these conflicts is as follows:

1. It is important to keep in mind that there is little or nothing more important than your relationship. If you remember that on a one to ten scale the importance of the relationship is an eleven while whatever you are conflicted about is below a ten, you are unlikely to do dumb things that place the relationship at risk in order to gain something of far less importance.

2. Remember that the person you are engaging in this conflict with is someone you love and cherish. Be sure that everything you do and say is consistent with this fact.

3. Despite numbers one and two above, you do not always have to "give in" to the other person in the interest of peace and harmony. People who do this can harbor a bit of resentment each time. Small resentments can pile up and become big resentments with dire consequences.

4. Engaging with the other person to resolve a conflict and being tough on issues but tender to the person you love

actually builds a relationship. The more conflicts the two of you successfully resolve in a positive manner, the greater the trust and confidence you will have in each other. Your track record will give you both confidence that you will be able to handle whatever comes next. In the real world of human relationships, there will always be something next.

5. If you have become the world's greatest expert on the person you love, you will know when, where, and how to address a conflict to maximize the possibility of a positive outcome. You will also know the triggers that set your loved one off, and you will strenuously avoid them.

6. Conflict management is a skill that needs to be developed. Remember the ten thousand hours required to master a skill? Practice good conflict management skills on minor conflicts so that the skills will be there to handle major conflicts.

7. Remain future focused. Nothing can be done to change the past. The past is only valuable to teach us what to do in the

present to create a more desirable future. If, for example, you are frustrated by the fact that your partner is chronically late for important events, you could rant about the past, or you could simply state that you find lateness extremely unpleasant and you would like to figure out a way that in the future this problem will go away. The other person can only be defensive about the past, so a conversation that dwells on the past is unlikely to go well. A conversation about what can be done about the future has a much higher probability of success.

8. If the temperature of the conversation is rising toward the point of ignition, you might want to cool things off a bit. Resolving a sticky problem in one sitting is often unrealistic. Remember this is a person you love and want to have a loving relationship with forever. In all that you do or say, remind him or her of that also.

9. Most problems that appear to be one big problem are often many small problems bundled together. Unbundling the

problem and resolving each of the small problems one by one is often the most productive approach.

A good friend of ours compares this to trying to break a bundle of sticks as opposed to unbundling the sticks and breaking them one by one. Good questions and listening skills are needed to identify the many small problems. Good questions and good listening is also very effective for turning the temperature of an argument down. Lots of practice with these two skills in non-conflict situations will ensure that the skills are there when you need them.

10. Ultimatums are relationship kryptonite. Stay away from them except as a last resort on an issue that must be resolved or the relationship is going to end anyway.

11. In a perfect world, all conflict would be satisfactorily resolved. In the real world, many conflicts are never resolved.

12. Constructive confrontation is an essential relationship skill. In a love

relationship, this skill is needed to gently and lovingly let the other person know about things that bother you or perhaps are detrimental to him or her.

13. There are certain things that no one but a lover is ever likely to be willing to confront about. Who else is going to tell you that you have spinach between your teeth, you need a shower, or that you look ridiculous in that workout outfit and do it in a way that is not attacking or cruel? OK, sometimes it is even a little cruel, but it is still better than allowing you to go out in public only to learn later that you looked ridiculous.

14. Avoid locking in on two competing solutions. When we "lock in" on two solutions, yours and mine, someone must win and someone must lose. We could argue for hours until one of us wears down and "gives in" in the interest of peace, but what does this do to the relationship? A far better approach is to expand the list of possible solutions to include many options and then to discuss the criteria we will use to select the best

option for both of us. This is the essence of the proverbial win-win solution.

15. Important conflicts can produce energetic discussions with a lot of feeling in them. If it ever gets to the point that you are on the verge of angry name calling, insults, or angry displays, go back to point one above.

Kids: a source of conflict and joy

Many years ago when our children were causing us some minor grief, one of us asked the other what to do, and the reply was "don't ever have kids." Since then we have jokingly used the phrase with parents whenever their children are being problematic.

The choice to have or not to have children—and, if so, how many—is a major one. The results of the decision touch every aspect of the relationship. This is why the conversation should happen before the relationship gets too far down the road. We know loving couples with proven long-term relationships who span the spectrum from no children to many, so there is no one formula.

For us, raising children is one of the greatest joys and one of the greatest challenges in our life. "Blended" families like ours are supposed to be even more challenging. Our kids fortunately have treated each other as siblings from the beginning of our relationship, and we have made all three "ours." This has worked well for us, and I feel deeply blessed by the gift of two wonderful children my wife brought to our marriage.

The bond between a mother and a child is very special. It is visceral and primal. The connection goes so deep that it is wired into the brain and the heart. For these reasons, any conversation about parenting can go from rational to irrational very easily. While I no longer remember the particulars, I do remember that some of the biggest arguments in our marriage occurred early about how to raise our kids. Reports from other parents, especially parents of blended families, confirm that the children are a serious point of contention.

The resolution to the issues related to children is the same as the resolution to any issue in the relationship. Seek first to understand the other person's thoughts and feelings, share your own, and then search together for the resolution that will work for the two of you. Remember that if you manage your relationship well, you will have one another for many years after the children have gone off on their own.

One wonderful thing about building a deeply loving relationship between two people is that it generates surplus love that is more than ample to supply a brood of any size. My brother and his wife have a wonderful relationship and a blended family of eleven children. Their love for each other created an abundance that they have lavished on their children, grandchildren, and great-grandchildren from a seemingly bottomless reservoir.

Differences in parenting practices can be a significant source of contention in the relationship. For several years I taught parenting courses. I did this while our kids were very young. As they grew older, I became less and less convinced that I knew anything about parenting. I still find parenting a humbling experience even though our children are adults, because each child is different and they change over time, so there is no one-size-fits-all approach that is likely to produce consistent results.

There is significant benefit from parents taking parenting training together or reading the same book and discussing what they have read. The benefit comes from discussing parenting topics and arriving at a common understanding regarding key parenting issues.

When the kids are misbehaving, the last thing that is needed is for the parents to start misbehaving. The course that I taught was parent effectiveness training (P.E.T.) based on the work of Thomas Gordon. I do not think the course is taught widely any longer, but I recommend Gordon's book with the same title.

One of our wonderful friends read an article that suggested that two people should raise puppies together first. The article said that the two should only consider having children together if they were able to raise the pups to be well-behaved dogs. Many years later the couple is still childless, even though I believe the two of them would have made excellent parents. So be careful about what you read and in particular what you take seriously, including everything in this book.

How to go from zero to stupid in ten seconds or less

Anger is the stuff that results in restraining orders, broken crockery, front page news, and ruined lives. Rarely does anger do any good, and often it results in tragic outcomes. It also is likely that you will become more intensely angry with the person you love or about something related to the person you love than anything else on earth.

Things done in an angry moment can end a relationship forever, so managing anger well is an essential aspect of managing conflict in the most important relationship in your life.

If you are going to beat anger, you are going to have to hang in there with me through an explanation of three critical phenomena:

1. The source of our anger reaction
2. The fact that anger is a secondary emotion
3. The layers of our brain and how anger lives in the stupid part

The Source

The first thing to know is that our reaction to any situation is not outside of us. It comes from inside of us. If, for example, you show an edible insect to both an average American and a person for whom this insect is a delicacy, you are likely to get a "yuck" and a "yum." The thought in one mind is unpleasant and in the other pleasant. The sight of the insect is neutral. What each person does with that sight determines the reaction. One way of thinking about this is to use an ABC model in which A is the activating event, B is our belief system about the activating event, and C is the consequent reaction we have based on our belief.

We can change our consequent reaction of C by changing our thoughts and beliefs about the situation B while doing nothing to change the activating event we are experiencing in A.

To understand this model, consider this example:

You are in the airport waiting for your flight home after a long and grueling business trip. You hear an announcement on the PA system that the flight has been cancelled and all passengers should go to customer service to be booked on a different flight. You comply and find a line of about two hundred people in front of you moving very slowly. Inside you are doing a slow boil since you know you are powerless, and in your mind the flight was probably half empty so they cancelled it to save money and fill other flights.

All of a sudden a guy elbows his way to the front of the line, and for some reason the agent takes him instead of telling him to go to the end of the line. You have enough control to not go "postal" and get hauled away by TSA, but all the time you are in line you build up more and more steam. You work carefully to get the exact agent that took the "line cutter," and you go on a rant about the airline, the agent, and the jerk who cut the line.

The agent then informs you that the "line cutter's" mother is dying and that if he did not get on a plane immediately, he would probably miss the opportunity to see her one last time.

Notice that the reality that your flight is cancelled and you had to wait in a long line to be further inconvenienced by a long wait for the next flight (A) has not changed, but what is going on inside your head (B) has changed, and therefore your anger level (C) has also changed. We can change the story we tell ourselves about what other people do and by so doing have control over our reaction. Please note that this is dirt simple but incredibly hard to do in practice. Give yourself ten thousand hours to get good at it.

A Secondary Emotion

The second thing to understand is that anger is always a secondary emotion that follows an emotion we do not want to have or do not want others to know that we have. Anger follows so quickly that we may not ever be fully conscious of the primary emotion unless we stop and think about it.

Anger rapidly follows feelings of helplessness, inadequacy, embarrassment, envy, and the like. In the example above, a flight cancellation is incredibly frustrating because you have no control or recourse whatever. So you might feel screwed, helpless, and frustrated in addition to being tired, disappointed, and many other things.

The next time you are the least bit angry, peel the layers back and examine the primary emotions that give rise to the anger. Often the anger evaporates as soon as you know what is really going on. Even when it still exists, it is easier to manage.

Brain Layers

The human brain is built in three layers. The most primitive layer is identical in form and function to the brains of all reptiles. If you cut this part of the human brain out and examined it next to a reptile brain of the same size, they would be hard to tell apart. The second layer of the human brain is the layer we have in common with all mammals. It provides the same functions in humans, dolphins, apes, and horses. Finally, there is the layer that makes us uniquely human. It is where all of the higher intellectual functions live. When we "go ballistic," blood drains from the upper two layers and gets delivered to the lizard brain.

When this happens we are functionally a lower life form with the intelligence and interpersonal skills of a lizard. While in this state we are likely to lash out verbally and perhaps even physically. While in this state we are not equipped to drive a car, make life decisions, or to have a loving conversation. A padded soundproof cell is the best place for us, but most home builders have not appreciated the need for such a room yet.

When one person "lizards out," it is important for him or her to have a recovery strategy. Couples who intend to have a long-term relationship would do well to work out ways for one lizard to not trigger the second lizard and for the remaining human to guide the lizard to safety.

"Anxiety is love's greatest killer. It makes others feel as you might when a drowning man holds on to you. You want to save him, but you know he will strangle you with his panic."

—Anaïs Nin

Love Lesson Eighteen

Tame the Green-Eyed Monster

Fearing the loss of your love to another can be viewed in two very different ways. The first says that jealousy is a function of your insecurity. If your relationship is strong and you are not suffering from feelings of inadequacy, then there is nothing to get upset about when your wife is talking to another man or your husband is talking to another woman.

The second says that this relationship is the most important aspect of your life and you are unwilling to let anything jeopardize it. From this perspective, jealousy and possessiveness are just a statement of how important the relationship is to you, and your guarding of it is merely prudence in action.

I currently believe that the truth probably includes both perspectives. In the early days of our relationship, the green-eyed monster of jealousy reared its ugly head a few times, and I handled the beast badly. I still regret the anger I showed then. As our relationship deepened and solidified, and as I grew up a bit more, I have been able to keep that monster in its cage, but I still am strongly protective when it comes to any threat, real or imagined, to the relationship I care so deeply about.

My wife and I have talked about this at length (notice a pattern here), and we both now know how to avoid circumstances that are likely to make the other uncomfortable. We also have ways of communicating in the moment to keep things from spiraling out of control.

Both parties have a responsibility to manage this beast.

"I can't really change my life to accommodate people who are jealous. I don't see why I should."

—Sting

Love Lesson Nineteen
Deal With the Envy of Others

If you build a blissful relationship, there will be people who are envious, resentful, and hateful to you. There are far too many sad, angry, bitter, and envious people in the world. Misery, unfortunately, loves company.

We discussed using a pen name to write this book so that we could avoid the backlash we are sure to get from some people. I use the word "we" here because while I am pressing the keys on the keyboard, my bride is my inspiration, editor, coach, mentor, and in all respects partner in this book and all other things. Some people will read the last sentence and gag. I feel sad for them.

Until writing this book, we have tried to be low key around others, especially couples who do not have a good relationship. Around our best friends we are ourselves because, as you might remember, we limit our friends to happy couples who have good relationships and therefore have nothing to get envious about. If you succeed in developing a deeply loving romantic relationship, and if you maintain it and strengthen it, you will suffer some backlash from envious people. Out of kindness to yourself and them, you might want to tone it down in their presence.

PART SIX

Till Death Do Us Part

In this part we will address the fact that one desirable outcome of all that we covered above is a lifelong relationship with the person we love. Given that life expectancies are increasing, it is not inconceivable that our children will have the potential for a marriage that could last seven decades or more. In this part we will cover the final three love lessons:

LL20.   It's a Marathon, Not a Sprint

LL21.   Growing Old Together is the Idea

LL22.   Lessons Applied Matter

"Love is not a
sprint, it's a
marathon, a
relentless pursuit
that only ends
when she falls
into your arms -
or hits you with
the pepper
spray."

—Wolowitz

The Big Bang Theory

Love Lesson Twenty

It's A Marathon, Not a Sprint

Getting into the top 16 percent of all loving couples and staying there is not something that will happen automatically. You will need to do everything in your power every day to nurture, support, and develop the relationship.

If you are like us and now enjoy a loving, caring relationship and do not want to be among the miserable majority, there are a few things you can do.

First, a relationship is easier to build and maintain than it is to fix when it is broken. Loving the best way you know how today while learning how you will love better tomorrow is the preventive medicine that keeps a relationship healthy. Make yourself the best husband or wife possible and ensure that your growth matches your spouse's so that you do not outgrow each other.

Every one of us has a short list of things our partner can do to irreparably damage a relationship. Find out what is on that list and make darn sure you never get within a mile of any one of them.

When Hernan Cortez landed his conquistadores and engaged in battle with the Aztecs, he burned his ships to eliminate any possibility of retreat. Burn your ships to eliminate any possibility other than staying in the relationship and making it work. Some couples have far too many easy escape routes and therefore give up too easily.

Prevent "hot stove" learning. Hot stove learning refers to single trial learning that is never forgotten because it is so painful. If you touch a hot stove once and get badly burned, you will not need to learn that lesson a second time. This kind of learning happens in relationships when one party hurts the other. Get outside help before you become the hot stove. Breaking up is a permanent solution to something that may be a temporary problem. By avoiding a hot stove moment and getting on the path to fully restoring the relationship, you can manage your way through the short-term problem, and the relationship can become even stronger.

"Even after all this time, the sun never says to the earth, you owe me. Look what happens with a love like that, it lights the whole sky."

—Hafez

Love Lesson Twenty-One

Growing Old Together is the Idea

If your relationship is a success, and you have some good luck, you will be together a long time. By definition, you will get old together. During that time the world will change, you will change, and your spouse will change.

Each life stage—newlyweds without children, young marrieds with young children, middle age with older children, empty nesters, seniors who are grandparents and then great-grandparents—introduces new challenges and new joys. The focus of the relationship changes. Your prosperity may increase and decrease with career change and whatever good and bad fortune you may experience. You may also have changes in your health and well-being.

Change may produce a crisis. The Chinese characters that represent the word crisis are composed of the character for danger and the character for opportunity. Each life transition is capable of introducing both new dangers and new opportunities for your love relationship. The strength you build in the relationship will to a large measure determine how well the relationship weathers each storm.

Some of the change is under your control or influence. I have noticed that as people age they become caricatures of themselves. If you are a bitter, petty, nasty person, you become more so with time, and these qualities are displayed in the shape of your face and body. By contrast, if you are a happy, loving person, you take on a kind of radiance that glows wherever you are.

Fawn Weaver's book *Happy Wives Club* documents her interviews with happy couples around the world who had been together a minimum of twenty-five years. One finding that startled her was how much younger than their contemporaries the men and women in these couples appeared. They were filled with a vitality and energy that their less-loving counterparts lacked.

My wife and I have also noticed that some couples work hard to minimize the ravages of time while others don't. We have found that diet, exercise, mental stimulation, and relaxation preserve the capacity to enjoy an active, full life that allows us to do things that many contemporaries cannot. These same things seem to slow down the visible signs of aging as well.

As change happens, it is important to make adjustments. When our youngest child left for college, we decided it was time for me to change my career from one that required extensive travel to one that allowed me to come home each night. We believe that making that decision was the right one to continue to nurture and build our relationship during a major life transition to empty nesters.

As we began to contemplate the inevitable loss of some physical and perhaps mental capability due to age, and as we pondered our own mortality, we decided to take retirement on the installment plan so that we could put a few check marks on our bucket list together while we had our full physical and mental powers. This meant foregoing income in peak earning years, but it has provided us with wonderful life experiences together.

When I returned to the working world, I reentered with renewed vigor, having been completely refreshed by the time out. The time we had together in retirement came at a stage in life when many couples experience staleness in their relationship. We instead had an adventure of a lifetime filled with new experiences and incredible togetherness.

We have also begun to experience some of the decline that is inevitable with age. We are a half step slower on the tennis court and find it a bit more difficult to remember where the car keys are. We have found it harder to keep pounds off and easier to put them on. There are more wrinkles and gray hair, and there are aches and pains in the morning, but the compensation is that we enjoy an ever-deepening love and the greater peace that comes with experience.

All couples we have talked to about aging have reported some challenging years when hormonal changes play havoc with body and mind in both genders. They also report rough spots as one or the other went through an early, mid, or late life crisis. The ones with deeply loving relationships worked their way through these challenges, as did we.

Most of the loving couples we know have also been through major illnesses or injuries or both. In all cases the bonds they formed held strong during trying times.

No couple knows how many days or minutes remain before one or the other of them will be lost to death. The absence of this knowledge means that it is important to treat every moment as though it were the last. Living fully in the moment and fully in love maximizes our bliss and creates a life without regret. If you treat every moment as though it is the last, sooner or later you will be right.

If you want to make God laugh, tell him about your plans."

—Woody Allen

Love Lesson Twenty-Two

Lessons Applied Matter

People like to talk about lessons learned, but a wise man once taught me that the ones that matter are not the lessons learned but the lessons applied. As a refresher, all twenty-two are listed below.

If you have read this far in the book, first of all, thank you for the time and effort you have put in. While it is possible that just reading has planted seeds that will somehow miraculously sprout into something positive in the future, that is way too passive an approach for something as important as love.

At some point you have to do something with the information. If you kept notes during your reading, congratulations. You have the most important part of the book, which is not what was in the book but what was in your mind as you read the book.

To take action on part one, begin with improving your self-knowledge. In many cases this will lead to an awareness of needing to engage in self-improvement to become "Love-Ready." Love-readiness means that you are very clear about what is truly important for you to be happy in life. You know your values and your needs, and you have gone beyond the superficial to your core values. Love-readiness also means that you have wrestled your neuroses to the ground.

I am of the opinion that almost all human beings would benefit from life coaching, counseling, therapy, or whatever you want to call the process of working out the kinks that we all acquire through the process of going through childhood and our teen years. We could probably place all freshmen in high school in therapy for a year and skip school that year and be ahead of the game as a society.

If you are going to have a lasting relationship with a fantastic man or woman, you need to be a fantastic guy or gal. The Buddhists say, "When the student is ready, the teacher will appear." For our purposes I will reword that to, "When the lover is ready, his or her beloved will appear."

When I say fantastic guy, I do not mean someone who looks like John Hamm, has Bill Gates's money, debates string theory with Stephen Hawking, and is on the Dalai Lama's speed dial list. If such a guy existed, I have no idea how he would manage his ego.

By fantastic guy or gal, I mean someone who has made the most of his or her personality, career, interpersonal skills, and physical appearance, and who is a kind, thoughtful, generous, high-integrity human being relatively free of craziness. Most people can aspire to these qualities, and those who do are likely to find many wonderful men or women who will find them desirable.

When you are "love-ready," you also know clearly what you want and need from a partner.

When you are "love-ready," all you need to do is to get out into the world and spend time in the kinds of places doing the kinds of things that are likely to be compatible with the lover of your dreams. This leads us to part two of the book, which is all about finding your love.

When Willie Sutton, the famous bank robber, was asked why he robbed banks, he replied, "That is where the money is." I suppose that you could apply that logic and hang out near ladies rooms, but you might get arrested. A better option is to engage the world in ways that place you in contact with like-minded people involved in wholesome activities.

As you meet people, you will put all of your great interpersonal skills to work and will ask good questions and exercise your superb listening skills to get to know the man or woman behind the persona. In the worst case you will get to know some people who are a bad fit for you. You will know this because you have your musts and wants clearly defined. You will save yourself and them a lot of time by moving on when it is clear that the fit is not good.

Eventually you will find your soul mate. I am going to assume that what you want with this person is captured in the definition of a love relationship in part three, in which case you are ready for the rest of the book, which is all about how to build and continuously improve a love relationship.

Parts 3, 4, 5, and 6: Building and Nurturing a Love Relationship

Our definition of a love relationship:

A lasting, healthy, and positive intense feeling of mutual deep affection, respect, admiration, romance, and sexual attraction between two people that is continuously renewed and deepened.

Is this what you want? If not, what do you want? Write down your own definition.

Using whatever definition you have chosen, make two lists. On list one, list all the current forces in your life that are driving you toward making the definition above a reality. List two is all of the current forces in your life driving you away from making the definition above a reality.

Let's suppose you have a clear idea of the person you would like to have a lasting love relationship with. That would be a positive force in the first list above. Let's suppose that you are out of work and living in the guest bedroom in your parent's basement and riding your bicycle to the unemployment office. I'm guessing most of that stuff would make it onto list two.

If you do a good job of building the two lists, you will have a pretty good idea of where you stand today. Getting real about where you stand today is the first step toward the future.

You could use the twenty-two lessons as a checklist to take personal inventory. When you come up with a positive, put it on list one. The negatives go on list two.

When doing this exercise, remember that the forces can be internal or external. If, for example, you discover that you have met no new people in the last year because you are shy and awkward when meeting new people, then your shyness and awkwardness go on the negative force list.

Imagine a tug-of-war between forces on the negative list and forces on the positive list. Each item on each list is represented as a person in the tug-of-war. Living in your parents' basement could be represented by a Schwarzenegger-size guy on the negative side of the contest. Your quick wit could be represented by a Peewee Herman-size guy on the positive side. If the positive team is stronger than the negative team, they will drag the rope toward the lasting loving relationship side. If the negative side is stronger, you can imagine the outcome.

The game plan, therefore, consists of getting rid

of the big guys on the negative side and recruiting some real beef for the positive side. Here are the questions to ask yourself:

1. What can I do to build upon existing positive forces?

2. What can I do to add new positive forces?

3. What can I do to diminish some of the negative forces?

4. What can I do to eliminate some of the negative forces entirely?

When you have made a long list of possible actions, you might be tempted to do them all. This is probably a bad idea. You have only so much time, energy, money, willpower, etc., to make changes in your life. Apply your limited resources to only those items that have a big bang for their buck. So ask yourself, "Of all the things I could do on this list, which will have the greatest positive impact?"

When you have the answer to this question, create an action plan to move forward and establish a deadline for it to be attained. If the deadline is more than a few weeks out, be sure to have milestones with dates closer in. Let's suppose that getting a job comes up as the number one thing you could do. Securing a new job can take a long time, so break it down into smaller pieces, such as "get my resume brushed up and reviewed by someone who can and will give me good feedback this week."

When you have the first item in motion, ask yourself, "Will this be enough for me to be successful?" If the answer is no, then go back to the list and look for the next most potentially potent action step there. Repeat the planning process and repeat until you have either maxed out all of your resources or you are convinced your efforts are sufficient to get your tug-of-war team across the winner's line.

If you remember all the way back to love lesson eight, which was about what it would take to become a world-class lover, we covered the idea of having "grit."

"Grit is passion and perseverance for very long-term goals. Grit is having stamina. Grit is sticking with your future, day in, day out, not just for the week, not just for the

month, but for years, and working really hard to make that future a reality. Grit is living life like it's a marathon, not a sprint."

You might have to show some real grit to attain the goals you set and to make the improvements needed to be fully "Love-Ready," find the love of your life, and then build a deep, lasting love relationship. There will never be a time when you can rest on your laurels. Nurturing the relationship and keeping it strong while taking it to new levels is an ongoing process. The rewards come from the progressive realization of your goals. It is all about the journey, not the destination.

You will have setbacks and disappointments along the way that will tempt you to give up, get depressed, get angry, blame others, and a myriad of other unhelpful thoughts and actions. When you hit a setback, pick yourself up, dust yourself off, maybe lick your wounds, and feel sorry for yourself for a little while, and then get back on track.

Defeat is only possible if you give up. If you are still striving, the outcome is as yet unknown. Because people and relationships are unique, there can never be one template or game plan that will fit.

In the introduction I wrote:

"What got me to go forward was the thought that perhaps one or more people might find something in this book that would bring some love and joy into their life and their partner's life."

I hope you are one of those people. I wish you and your partner a lifetime of love.

LL1	Mistakes Hurt Others Too
LL2	You Need a "Why"
LL3	Choose Carefully and Well
LL4	Give Yourself a Chance
LL5	Decide Who is Out
LL6	And the Winner Is?
LL7	You Create Love by What You Do
LL8	Love is Simple, but It is Not Easy
LL9	Listen, Listen, Listen
LL10	Build Trust and Confidence
LL11	Create the Right Rhythm of Togetherness
LL12	Associate with Nurturing People
LL13	Open a Love Bank
LL14	Keep Withdrawals to a Minimum
LL15	Get on the Same Page and Stay There
LL16	Vulnerability is the Price You Must Pay
LL17	Manage Conflict Constructively
LL18	Tame the Green-Eyed Monster
LL19	Deal With the Envy of Others
LL20	It's a Marathon, Not a Sprint
LL21	Growing old Together is the Idea
LL22	Lessons Applied Matter

ABOUT THE AUTHOR

Terry McDonald is a philosopher servant. A philosopher because of his endless thirst for and love of wisdom and knowledge and a servant because he takes joy in serving others. He lives and loves with his wife in the beautiful and literary-minded town of Fairhope, Alabama.